Tibet

Between Heaven and Earth

Tibet
Between Heaven and Earth

Peter Grieder

Foreword by the Dalai Lama

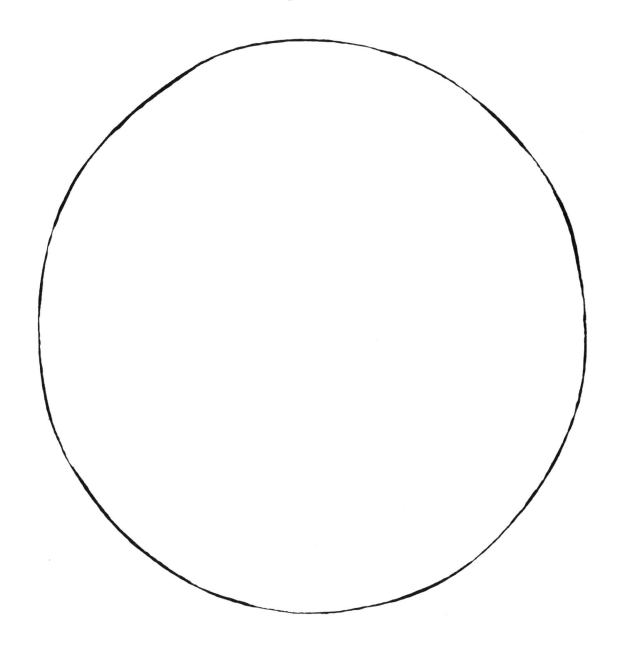

CLEAR LIGHT PUBLISHERS
SANTA FE, NEW MEXICO

This book is dedicated to all seekers

© La Renaissance du Livre, Tournai (Belgium)
for the first edition in French.
Copyright 2003 © Peter Grieder
All rights reserved.

Clear Light Publishers
823 Don Diego
Santa Fe, New Mexico 87505
www.clearlightbooks.com

First Edition
10 9 8 7 6 5 4 3 2 1

Library of Congress Cataloging-in-Publication Data

Grieder, Peter.
  Tibet : between heaven and earth : an inner journey / by Peter Grieder;
  with a foreword by the Dalai Lama.
      p. cm.
Includes bibliographical references and index.
  ISBN 1-57416-065-6
  1. Buddhism--China--Tibet. 2. Tibet (China)--Description and travel.
3. Buddhism--China--Tibet--Pictorial works. 4. Tibet
(China)--Pictorial works. 5. Himalaya Mountains Region--Pictorial
works. I. Title.
  BQ7604 .G75 2002
  951'.5--dc21

                                              2002010490

Front and back cover photographs © Peter Grieder.
Front and back endsheets: left—*One Thousand Buddhas* with Amitabha in the center;
right—*One Thousand Buddhas* with Manjughosha in the center, both from *The World of
Tibetan Buddhism*, © Gyosei Ltd., Japan.
Printed in Belgium.

THE DALAI LAMA

Modern improvements in travel and communications facilities have made the world a smaller place. We can now visit what were previously remote regions and meet the people who live there, or at least share the experiences through the photographs and accounts of those who have been there. In this way, we can increasingly appreciate how, despite differences of geography and culture, human beings are much the same. We are all trying to find happiness and avoid pain according to our circumstances, and in this way we are all very dependent on each other and on our environment.

Peter Grieder has traveled from his home in the mountains of Europe and found inspiration among the great Himalayas. What unites the people that he met in Ladakh, Zanskar, Bhutan and Tibet is a remarkable sense of fortitude and contentment derived largely from a common culture rooted in Buddhism.

One of the key elements of Buddhist teachings is the importance of the inner journey. No matter what external developments we may make in our world and or what magnificent things we may see in it, without a corresponding inner development we will not find the happiness we ultimately seek. However, if each of us can journey within and develop a warm heart towards others and calm in our minds, there lies real hope for peace and joy in the world.

Table of Contents

Introduction

This is a very personal book. It is the outcome of my own personal search for truth. In order to let the reader participate in my quest, I tried to put the photographs and texts together in such a way that an inner context, a kind of thread on which the beads are strung, is given. Following this sutra —this is the word in ancient India for "thread"—I would like to gradually guide the contemplative reader and observer from the outside to the inside, and would like to invite him/her on a journey with the aid of my own personal travel pictures.

The journey starts with images of flowers, lakes, children and landscapes. It ends with the *Tibetan Book of the Dead*. As in a mandala, the path begins on the periphery and ends in the guarded secret of the center.

I would like to make it clear in advance that I am not a Tibetologist. The justification to write about the "Land between Heaven and Earth," its culture and its religion, is based solely on my experience as the director of the Tibetan Monastic Institute in Rikon and on my own personal experience of life.

At this point, I would like to take the opportunity to thank all the people who have accompanied me on my way through life. Without their support this book would never have been written.

When the time comes that iron birds can fly and horses roll on wheels,
The man from the land of snow will have to leave his homeland, fleeing like ants
And the doctrine will spread to the land of the red-faced people."
—Padmasambhava, prophecy dating from the 8th century

1 • The founder of the Dharma, Siddharta Gautama Buddha.

Departure for the Himalayas
Land and People

Ethnic Tibet

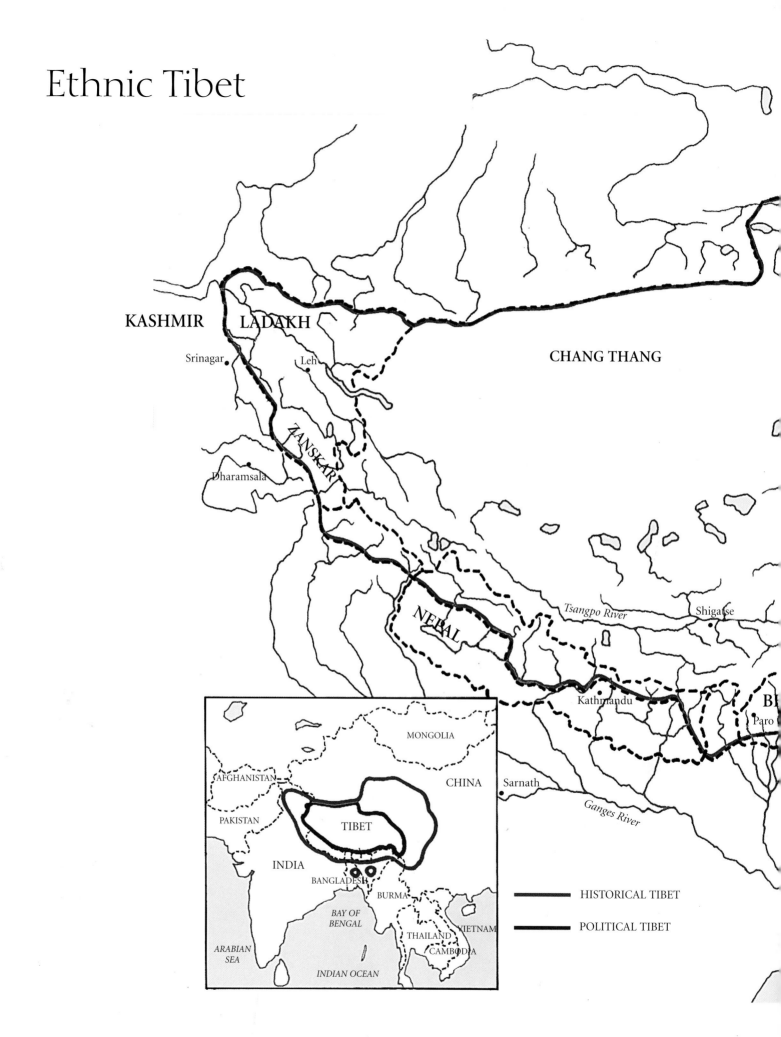

KASHMIR LADAKH CHANG THANG

Srinagar Leh

ZANSKAR

Dharamsala

NEPAL

Tsangpo River Shigatse

Kathmandu B

Paro

Sarnath

Ganges River

MONGOLIA

AFGHANISTAN CHINA

PAKISTAN TIBET

INDIA

BANGLADESH

BURMA

BAY OF
BENGAL VIETNAM

THAILAND
CAMBODIA

ARABIAN
SEA

INDIAN OCEAN

——————— HISTORICAL TIBET

——————— POLITICAL TIBET

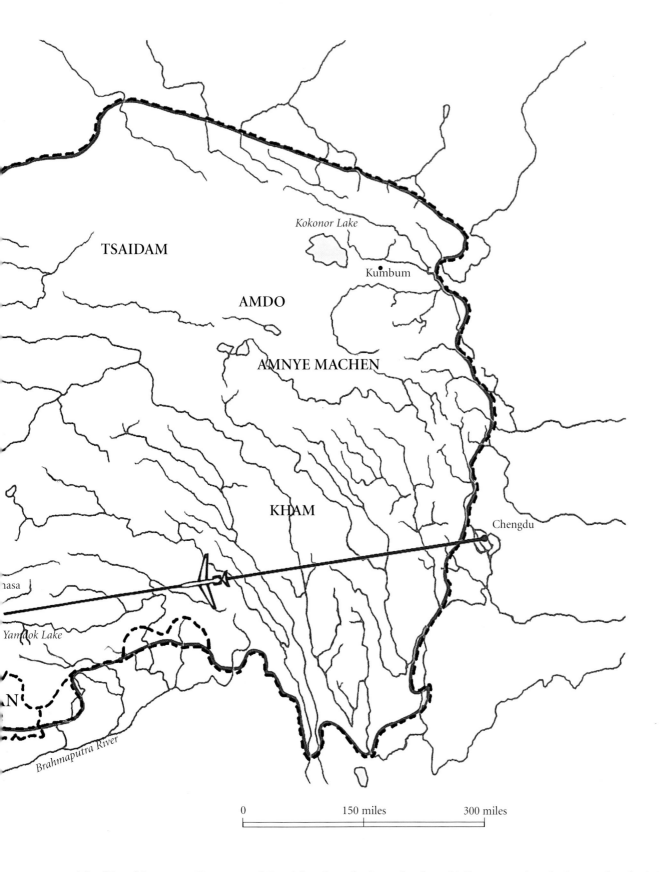

The "Land between Heaven and Earth"—the ethnic and cultural Tibet—reaches far beyond today's political borders that were randomly set by the Chinese rulers. It reaches from the Himalayan mountains in the south to the deserts of Inner Asia in the north and from the rugged valley of the Karakorum mountains in the west all the way into the provinces Qinghai and Gansu in the northeast (Amdo), including Sichuan and Yunnan in the east (Kham). This book is about the historical Tibet.

The Lotus—Symbol of Purity

As pure and untouched as a virgin, the lotus bud grows towards the cool morning sky. The future is only just an idea, but perfection has already been determined deep within. The day, the hour, is approaching in which it will open, unfold and fully blossom towards the light. Immaculate, it will triumph over the mud and the dirt out of which it has grown, yet which is its maternal, fertile soil.

Is it this unshakeable trust that ultimately everything will take a turn for the better; is it this basic faith in existence, in being as it is, that has blessed the people of the "Land between Heaven and Earth" with something that we perceive again and again as "heartfelt joy"?

2 • *A lotus bud, pure and untouched like a virgin, grows towards a new day.*

3 • A fully blossomed lotus—symbol of purity and the triumph of the unsullied True Nature of man over the sludge of the world.

Kashmir

The road to "Little Tibet" leads through the enchanting mountain valley of Kashmir

Traveling by land from the plains of Northern India to Ladakh takes you through the magnificent "Vale of Kashmir." The Kashmir basin, famous for its lakes, lies at an altitude of approximately 5,600 feet and is the largest high-mountain valley in the Himalayas.

The capital, Srinagar, surrounded by rice paddies, poplar forests and saffron fields, is situated on the banks of the Jhelum River, right next to the lotus-covered Dal Lake. Although it can get quite cold in the winter months—the waterways can freeze over and winter sports take place in Gulmarg—the valley is actually located on the border of the subtropical climate zone. This combined with the altitude creates an absolutely ideal climate for summer vacationers. On the one hand, it is nice and summery for the sun worshippers from the north, and on the other hand, it is wonderfully cool for the Indians who are troubled by the heat! In any case, the Kashmiri people themselves are convinced that God created paradise here…

The Kashmiris live according to the laws of the Koran

The teachings of Lord Buddha are said to have reached Kashmir as early as the 3rd century B.C., during the reign of the Emperor Ashoka. However, the contemporary inhabitants of this mountain valley are Muslims. They have been immigrating in different waves from the west since the 10th century. Their production of carpets, the craft for which they are still famous today, leads us to believe that they originally came from Persia and Turkestan.

Although the Islamic tradition in the Himalayas has somewhat adapted itself to the Hindu and Buddhist traditions, the fundamental features of the faith in the Prophet Mohammed remain basically unchanged. But among the Muslim conquerors of Kashmir were many Sufis, members of the mystical order of Islam. The following poem by the Persian poet Jalal al Din Rumi (13th century) shows just how closely related the mystics of all religions are on the inner plane. Doesn't the following touch on the Eastern beliefs of evolution and reincarnation?

> *I died as a stone and became a plant,*
> *I died as a plant and became an animal,*
> *I died as an animal and became a man.*
> *Therefore, why should I be afraid of death?*
> *Was I ever worse or inferior when I died?*
> *At one point, I will die as a man and*
> *become a being of light, an angel of the dream.*
> *But my path continues:*
> *Everything disappears except God;*
> *I will become the star amongst all the stars*
> *and will shine over birth and death.*

4 • *A lake covered with lotuses in the mountain valley of Kashmir. The Kashmiris are convinced that God created paradise here.*

5 • *A young Kashmiri on the way to the floating vegetable market with his merchandise.*

6 • Present-day
inhabitants of the
valley between the
Himalayas and the
Karakoram are
Muslims who have
been immigrating in
different waves from
the west since the 10th
century and have
driven out Buddhism.
This is a Kashmiri
mother dressed in an
Indian sari in a park
near the capital of
Srinigar.

Bargaining is the joy of the Kashmiris

If you have never in your life haggled with a Kashmiri about the price of a carpet, you cannot really know a Kashmiri! These people have been passionate traders since they were knee-high, and their tricky negotiation tactics, their persistence and their often wily craftiness are beyond what even most seasoned travelers have ever experienced. Even the Tibetans, known throughout the Himalayas as good traders and tough negotiators, think twice before closing a deal with a Kashmiri. From the point of view of the Kashmiris, bargaining is an expression of their zest for life. It is a game, a sport; to win is a matter of honor—and ultimately a question of self-respect. There is no better way to impress a Kashmiri than by actually being able to turn the duel in one's own favor through even greater shrewdness and persistence.

In order to get from Srinagar to Leh, the capital of Ladakh, you must travel by jeep or bus. This journey, by no means easy or safe, takes you over three notoriously dangerous passes: the Zoji-La, the Namika-La and finally the Fatu-La. Near Mulbekh there is a Maitreya Buddha hewn out of rock and as tall as a house. This is where the ethnic and cultural Tibet starts, and the password is no longer "Inshallah" (May Allah's will be done) but "Lha-gyel-lo" (Victory to the Gods!).

7 • There is probably no place in the world where merchants are more persistent and crafty than in Kashmir. Here a merchant is selling salt that comes from one of many salt lakes in Tibet and has always been a traditional export of the Tibetans.

Ladakh

8 • *The Zoji-La, or the "pass of the four snake spirits," is one of the most treacherous passes between the Himalayas and the Karakoram. Every summer trucks, buses and jeeps fall over the side of the road.*

9 • *Twenty-two hairpin curves lead from Fatu-La, the "pass into the next world," down into the upper reaches of the Indus River.*

Agriculture in the arid mountain wilderness of Ladakh

Situated between the Himalayan and the Karakoram ranges, most of Ladakh is a high desert. But efficient irrigation in the valleys facilitates a sort of oasis-like farming as the runoff from snowmelt and glaciers flows down in the spring and early summer. The intensity of the sun is similar to that of the southern Mediterranean and explains why summer barley can be planted up to an altitude of almost 15,000 feet. Peas, beans and winter vegetables thrive under these conditions; even apricots and peaches are able to ripen in protected places.

Still, the growing season is very short. The soil can only be cultivated between the end of May and the middle of August. Because of the altitude and sun's intensity, this short period is just long enough for the crops to ripen. The only grain that really thrives at this altitude is barley. It has a pleasant taste but has the disadvantage of not containing any gluten, which means that one cannot make bread from it, not even unleavened bread. The local people roast the barley on hot stones and then grind it into a flour. Tsampa, the staple diet of the Tibetans, is prepared by mixing the roasted flour with butter, tea and a bit of salt.

10 • Although the high desert is arid, a stable agricultural economy is possible. Runoff from snowmelt and glaciers and the intense sun facilitate cultivation of barley and winter vegetables up to an altitude of almost 15,000 feet.

The peoples of the Himalayas

There is hardly another place in the world with a population as diverse as that of the Himalayan countries. In addition to the Kashmiris who immigrated from the Near East, the light-skinned Dards in the west, the Dolpa living between Nepal and Tibet, the Lepcha from Sikkim and the *Monpa* and *Naga* people at the eastern end of the mountain chain, two dozen other tribes could probably be mentioned. Some have only a few thousand members. The Sherpas (the "people from the east"), who immigrated from Eastern Tibet to Nepal, have established a worldwide reputation as mountain guides and indispensable porters for mountain expeditions. The large tribe of the Bhutia, originally from Tibet, are now settled in the neighboring states of Nepal, Sikkim and Bhutan as nomads, merchants and farmers.

The Tibetans are divided into two very distinct groups. One group consists of the rather small inhabitants of the southern central provinces of U and Tsang, friendly, jolly people with moon-shaped faces (see opposite photograph). The other group, the tall and proud warrior people, consists of the Amdowa from the northeastern province of Amdo and the Khampas from the rugged mountains of Kham in the east. Their sharply cut features and aquiline noses remind one of Native Americans (see image 65). All of them have been marked by the hard outdoor life in the mountains: they are hardworking, reliable, tough—and clever. Ethnology notwithstanding, the Tibetans know who their ancestors were: a forest monkey and a rock goddess, and that, over time and due to different food, they lost their tails and their fur…

11 • *Trees are rare in this high desert. Wherever there is a small cluster of trees, mostly poplars and willow, there is water and thus a human settlement.*

12 • A young girl with her decorated felt hat looks shyly into the camera of the foreign photographer.

13 • The Ladakhis are ethnic Tibetans, and both their facial features and their mentality differ markedly from those of the Kashmiris who immigrated from the Near East. A typical trait of the Ladakhis is their radiant good humor.

14 • *A good hat, protection against the strong sun, is more important at this altitude than a good pair of pants.*

15 • The arrival of a foreigner with all his gear and baggage always creates a sensation in the remote Zanskar valley.

16 • A typical village in the Zanskar Valley (13,850 feet). The precious fuel, thornbushes and yak dung, is carefully stacked on the roofs of houses.

17 • Mothers carry their children in colorful wraps tied around their backs. Don't these naturally dyed cloths, this closeness of the infants, this tranquility also indicate a good quality of life?

How will the new road affect the inhabitants of the Zanskar Valley?

Only a few years ago, the Zanskar Valley, the large valley of the Upper Indus region, was opened up by the construction of a road. Until that time, the inhabitants of this region hardly had any contact with the people "on the other side of the mountain." Getting to the larger settlements, such as Kargil and Leh, implied going on an arduous trek that took weeks. During the winter months even this was impossible, unless the traveler risked finding a way across the treacherous ice of the frozen rivers. There is still a sign on the only mailbox in the Zanskar Valley, in the main town of Padum, that reads, "Mail collection next summer!"

The poor yet far from miserable inhabitants live together peacefully in this remote region. They feel protected within their extended families. The sky and the earth, mountains and flowers, children and animals determine their lives. Their desires barely go beyond the basics of everyday life, and they are hardly aware of how extremely difficult their living conditions are since they have never experienced anything else. Are these people really happy? Some think it's certain; others argue that the inhabitants of this valley should be freed from their isolation and given material aid. In the end, the Indian Parliament granted them a loan to construct a mountain road approximately 200 kilometers long.

What has this "road"—which often looks more like a riverbed—really done for the Zanskaris? During the summers, a few hundred visitors make the arduous, dusty, three-day journey to Padam. They bring with them blue jeans, transistor radios, watches and the like, providing business opportunities for the young, enthusiastic Zanskaris who parade around wearing the latest style sunglasses. These young people hope for a better standard of living through contact with the Western industrial world, while the elders are worried that the consequences will be restlessness and greed, the disintegration of ancient traditions and loss of their quality of life. Who is right?

It's a question being argued about all over the world, the answer to which is so difficult because the problem is not really an economic one but one of a philosophy of life. Aren't people always happy when they are *satisfied* with whatever they have, even if it is very little? Our own experience has taught us that *unfulfilled* desires create unhappiness, no matter how much we already possess.

The new road has opened the door of our world to the Zanskaris and thus the door to a materialistic way of thinking. We know only too well what degree of happiness it has brought to us. Yet, they now have to experience this new influence *on their own.*

We know the parable of the "prodigal son." The father did not prepare a feast for the son who stayed dutifully at home but for the other son, who had ventured out into the turbulent world and, richer in experience, found his way back home.

18 • *Although barefoot and in rags, this elderly man makes his way with dignity to a religious gathering.*

The relationship between the monasteries and the lay population

Although Ladakh is part of India, it is a region in which many traditions rooted in Tibetan culture continue unchanged. In the old days, at least one out of seven children had to dedicate his life fully to the quest for truth. The other six were responsible for the livelihood of this privileged one. This is how the monastic communities started, and the population still feels deeply responsible for this support.

Since girls and women, as in most cultures, are only rarely prepared to renounce the family for monastic life (in a nunnery), it is more common for one out of five rather than seven boys to be brought to the monastery for his education. These boys are free to take off their monk's robes at any time, but they tend to remain in the monastery for the rest of their lives, and the families still today support the monastic community with food and clothing. Blood ties are of the utmost importance in this ancient culture and thus the families maintain close contact with their relatives in the monastery.

In return, monks on the "path to enlightenment" commit themselves to teaching the lay population in many different ways and to caring for their spiritual needs.

19 • A high incarnate lama (tulku) is traveling through the valley, giving spiritual teachings. On the right are the married women recognizable by their beautiful headdresses (perak); on the left are the unmarried girls.

The significance of monasteries for Tibet and its culture

Before the destruction of thousands of places of worship during the Chinese Cultural Revolution, there were probably as many monasteries in Tibet in relation to the number of inhabitants as there are schools in Western countries. They ranged in size from the smallest village gompa to the mighty state monasteries, comparable to our universities, near the Tibetan capital of Lhasa. During their more than one-thousand-year history, the monasteries were the absolute center of the Tibetan culture. Not mere places of religious thought and worship but powerful educational institutions, they were the custodians of the arts such as painting, calligraphy and music, as well as centers of scientific exploration in medicine and astrology. There was hardly any field of knowledge that did not fall under the auspices of the monasteries.

These institutes have an additional social function; they offer talented young men, regardless of their social status or background, the possibility to rise socially. Within the strictly structured hierarchy of the monastery, each individual basically has the same chance to attain an exalted position. As an abbot of one of the large state monasteries, one could even have a say in government issues. In the 13th century, under the reign of the Mongols who then ruled all of Central Asia, the abbot of the Sakya monastery was not only the head priest of the Tibetan Buddhist world, but also the prince and royal regent of Tibet. Similarly, the 14th Dalai Lama, who has been living in exile in India since 1959, is the religious and worldly head of the Tibetans.

20 • As cultural strongholds which are still intimately tied to the religion, the monasteries are of great importance to the Ladakhis. This is the monastery of Tikse, which was built between 1410 and 1440.

21 • *The monastery of Lamayuru is situated far above the Indus valley, just off the Srinagar-Leh road.*

22 • *A novice monk (getsul) of the monastery of Lamayuru. Until a few years ago the monasteries were the only places where boys could get an education.*

The Tibetan script and language

King Songtsen Gampo, who lived in the 7th century and according to tradition was the 32nd king of Tibet, had two wives. One of them, Wen-ch'ing, belonged to the family of the Chinese emperor, while the other wife, Bhrikuti, was a princess of the royal house of Nepal. Both were devoted Buddhists and convinced their husband to introduce Buddhism into his kingdom.

It is assumed that, at that time, the Tibetan language was a dialect with no written script. In order for the teachings of the Buddha to be translated, a script had first to be developed. King Songtsen Gampo sent one of his ministers to India with instructions to develop an appropriate script and grammar derived from Sanskrit.

Since Sanskrit belongs to the Indo-Germanic language family like Greek and Latin, a connection exists between Tibetan script and that of our language family. For example, Tibetan script is written horizontally from left to right and not vertically, as one would expect from a language that belongs to the Chinese language family.

This beautiful script, very demanding from a calligraphic point of view, has basically three variations—block letters, cursive writing and numerous more or less stylized forms. Since until recent times only religious texts were written and printed, the script has remained the same, right down to the smallest detail.

23 • A young monk is practicing an ornamental script that is beautiful as well as demanding from a calligraphic point of view. Using a wooden stick that he moistens again and again with his mouth, he is tracing the syllables on a black wooden board that has been covered with a thin layer of chalk.

24 • *The magnificent frescos in the monasteries are not intended merely as decorations. They have always primarily had symbolic significance. This is the enchanting image of a Bodhisattva, making the gesture* (mudra) *of fearlessness and protection* (abhaya mudra) *that encourages others to approach him.*

The meaning of paintings and ritualistic music

In the entire Tibetan cultural area, artistic impulses are rooted in religious experience. They bring inner experiences to a subtle, tangible plane, making them accessible to the senses. The inner visions are reflected in the tantric Buddhist works of art. In the Tibetan tradition, they are divided into *kuten* (body receptacle—for example, a statue), *sungten* (speech receptacle) and *thugten* or *chorten* (mind or receptacle for the senses).

Kuten (body) in the widest sense indicates the outer material manifestation of a work of art. In its highest form, art can be compared to a bell cast for the spiritual to manifest on the worldly plane. And sungten (speech) can be understood as the metallic sound the bell awakens in us. In this context, chorten (meaning) indicates the absolute balance between form and content. Again, within this balance, the work of art forms a bridge to the spiritual realm. The shapes, colors, rhythms, sounds and symbols, architecture of the monasteries, paintings, poetry and music all express one common aim—to allow a person to grow spiritually and find liberation.

Although, traditionally, famous artists were commissioned by wealthy patrons to create works of art for ritual purposes, this type of creativity remained essentially anonymous. Most important was not the artist as a person, but the formalized message of the work of art, its symbolic purpose. Even though the artist was highly regarded, he was not revered. He was, however, not merely a craftsman; he understood himself as a vessel for suprapersonal inspiration. In an Indian temple complex there is a magnificent statue and in the pedestal the anonymous sculptor chiseled the following words: "How in the world did I do this!" The humility of that artist is characteristic. It was not the impulse for creative freedom that inspired the creator of the wonderful fresco of a *Bodhisattva* (image 24). Most of the details, such as the position of the hands and feet, the jewelry and choice of colors, were already set by the iconographical tradition and did not allow the artist any artistic freedom, especially since the painting of the image was almost certainly commissioned. And yet, simply good craftsmanship could never have produced an image with such a radiant energy. The prescribed gesture (mudra) of the right hand means: "Come closer and do not be afraid." It is emphasized by the utterly gentle and loving facial expression. The image moves one deeply because the form and the message correspond.

Perhaps this example conveys especially well why the art of the peoples from the Himalayas is so timeless. This art form is rarely decorative; instead it is mainly instructive and aims at evoking the highest forms of contemplation and meditation; its innermost intention is to make the eternally valid truths visible.

Wherever there is light, there is darkness. Wherever there is joy, there is suffering. Wherever there is loving kindness, there is rejection and hatred. This insight, usually completely repressed in most Western cultures, finds its full expression in Buddhist Tantra. This is why the terrifying, all-devouring Palden Lhamo rides on her ghost-mule across a lake of blood, spreading the plague. Her head is surrounded by an aureole of fire and crowned with skulls; she is seated on human skins, and the sinister eye on the croup of her mount is the iconographic confirmation that she is, indeed, the "unmentionable one." One of the eternally valid truths of our polar world is: All good things have an equally large shadow!

25 • The terrifying
Palden Lhamo on her
ghost-mule, with the
mysterious "third eye"
on its croup, is the
guardian of Lhasa, the
capital of Tibet. A
monk is busy repairing
the "lake of blood."

Music is also an important component of the Tibetan Buddhist rituals. This music is very unique and is used on a mystical level to direct positive and negative forces. The combination of bells, horns, oboes, cymbals and different drums creates a primordial world of sound which, at times, can give the listener chills. Rituals with bells, accompanied by the *dungkar* (a shell that is blown like a trumpet) and the *gyaling* (an instrument resembling an oboe) played in pairs, are used to activate the pacifying forces. Drum rituals, on the other hand, are meant to destroy the negative forces or at least keep them from producing evil. The most sinister and unusual instrument is the *kangling*, a horn made from a human thigh bone according to very precise instructions. Its eerie sound—zam-hum-ham-hohohoho—seems to go right through the listener. Here, too, the aim is to initiate a dynamic process of enlightenment. It's in hell that the longing for heaven is most intense.

26 • A young monk blows the dungchen, *an instrument similar to a Swiss alphorn.*

27 • *The annual festival in Phiyang is opened by the eerie, yet beautiful, deep sounds of the long copper horns: the Cham mystery plays can now begin.*

28 • *The movements of the Cham dancer, who is dressed in a sumptuous and flowing brocade costume, follow very precise instructions.*

The Cham mystery plays

Around the world, mystery plays are initiation rites that symbolize the battle between the forces of light and darkness. These plays always end with the good being victorious. Ultimately, the only reality is the light, darkness being light's shadow, the absence of light. In the past, this type of mystery play was celebrated in most of the lamaic monasteries at the time of the winter solstice.

Just like many of the mystical Swiss carnival customs that have been kept alive until today, especially in isolated mountain villages, the *Cham festival* originally celebrated the victory of the new year. Each day that lasted longer than the previous one was symbolic of the victory over the demonic forces of winter which were robbing the light. Today, this tradition is only alive in the regions bordering Tibet, such as Ladakh, Sikkim and Bhutan, and its performance date, calculated according to the lunar calendar, now falls mainly in the summer months.

The essential costumes for these colorful dances are precious flowing brocade robes. The wild-looking masked gods depict demons and animals. All of the ritual objects, such as daggers, choppers, bows and arrows, vajras (*dorje*), skull cups, etc., are part of the play. The dance steps and choreography follow precise instructions taken from very early Tantric Buddhist scriptures. Only monks are allowed to act out the roles in the performances, which consist mostly of pantomimes accompanied by music. These performances usually take place in the courtyard of the monastery.

For weeks, everyone in the monastery, adults as well as children, is preoccupied with the preparations for this annual festival. A few days before the festival, the performers go on a strict fast and meditate on the "emptiness" of all things. The night before the start of the festival, the masks are "brought to life" through special rituals. Accompanied by the thundering sounds of the "big horns" (*dungchen*) thirteen magicians of the Black Hat sect make their appearance, in order to ban all evil. Thirteen is the sacred number of the *Bon* tradition, indicating the pre-Buddhist origin of these dances. Imposing "monk-guards," armed with long white-washed sticks or horse whips, are responsible for peace and order amongst the multitude of visitors. Several "jesters" relish their free rein, making fun of even the sacred scenes. Their jokes and tricks cause people to laugh, livening up the almost frightening seriousness of the play.

For three entire days, interrupted only by short lunch breaks, the dancers perform almost constantly. Heroes of the ancient Tibetan mythology with rattles and drums make their appearance as do Indian Brahmins, who look silly with their stilted manner and mask. Wrathful guardian deities and Dharma protectors do ritual dances in the courtyard, followed by skeletons and masked ghosts carrying magical mirrors as protective shields against demons. Furies sweep across the courtyard dancing wildly, and screaming children make fun of an old Chinese scholar. This scene is supposed to symbolize the victory of Tibetan Buddhism over the Chinese scholars at the royal court in the 8th century. The dance of the stag mask, apparently only seen in Sikkim in earlier times, is one of the most brilliant dances due to the costumes consisting of brightly colored robes, shiny yellow masks and the colorful pennants tied between the antlers. Because of its expansive steps, high jumps and incredibly fast turns, this dance surpasses all others in its beauty and elegance.

In the end, the God of Death, Yama, defeats the small dough figure in the shape of a human lying in the middle of the courtyard, a scene that brings the pre-Buddhist blood sacrifices to mind. Yama stabs the figure to death with a ritual dagger, chops it up and eats part of it. Then, four skeletons perform a dance of joy, thus bringing to an end this very terrifying and impressive scene.

The Cham dances, still deeply rooted in pre-Buddhist thought, are mainly practiced by the Kagyu School, the unreformed order of the "Red Hats." The reformed monasteries of the Gelugpa tradition, of which the Dalai Lama is also a member, have a more reserved attitude towards these dances.

29 • ...turning and turning.

30 • A "Black Hat" magician performs a ritual that was probably a terrifying blood sacrifice in pre-Buddhist times. He is holding a ritual dagger, a phurbu, in his right hand.

31 • The "human sacrifice," nowadays made out of barley flour (tsampa) and butter since Buddhism has taken over these old customs, symbolizes a demon.

The old Bon rituals and Buddhism

Buddhism, being purely epistemological, does not have a concept of God such as we do, and is therefore not dogmatic. As a result, Buddhism has been able to assimilate the content of other religions without losing its own identity. This was the case with some of the old pre-Buddhist rituals from the Bon period that Buddhism was able to reinterpret. For example, one might ask how a ritual instrument like the dagger found a place in a religion as peaceful as Buddhism. In fact, the first commandment (*shila*) says: "I endeavor to cause no harm to any sentient being." We know that a demon, who embodies evil and must therefore be destroyed, is projected into the *lingam* (a figure of a human being made out of barley flour). However, from the Buddhist point of view, a demon is also a sentient being whom we need to protect and is therefore not killed. Rather, the Black Hat magician is specifically trained to destroy only the ignorance of the demon. Thus, the demonic creature itself is liberated. Only ignorance turns a "being" into a demon. "To kill" and "to liberate" therefore have the same meaning in specific Buddhist scriptures.

32 • A young girl's face already reflects her intense inner participation in the eerie, yet fascinating ritual.

33 • *The Ladakhi landscape is overwhelming and affects every visitor—people either love it or hate it.*

People between heaven and earth

We are standing at an altitude of 14,850 feet above sea level and the air is thin, not just because of the altitude, but also because there is no vegetation to produce oxygen. The silence here is eerie—no murmuring of a brook, no whistling of the wind in the branches of the trees. The glaring sun burns down mercilessly from the cloudless sky. Suddenly, without warning, a mass of humid air rises up from the Indian subcontinent and forms a menacing black wall of clouds. Flashes of lightning light up the sky. Hail beats down on the dried-out earth. Then, once again, the sun appears and silence reigns over the barren mountain wastes. This dreary moonscape is at once fascinating and terrifying. We feel like lost children standing between heaven and earth: helpless, defenseless, alone. And yet, at the same time, we feel close to both, aware of a blessed synthesis with heaven and earth. We feel an almost unbearable rift in our souls as an overpowering longing for a place of refuge arises in us.

Could that be the reason why in the course of centuries so many monastic communities have been formed in this hostile high desert landscape? A monastery promises protection and security, human warmth, colors, sounds, scents—and the "lost" human being can take refuge in the infinite Oneness that he or she is longing for. The traditional prayer of refuge to the "Three Precious Jewels" (*triratna*) according to all Buddhist schools is: "I take refuge in the *Buddha*, the *Dharma* (his teachings) and the *Sangha* (the Buddhist community)."

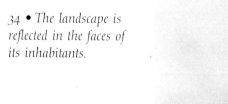

34 • The landscape is reflected in the faces of its inhabitants.

35 • *The legendary blue flower, the blue poppy, only blossoms in the isolated mountain valleys of the Himalayas.*

Bhutan

Bhutan, the "Land of the Dragons"

Druk-yul, "Land of the Dragons," is the only remaining Buddhist kingdom in the Himalayas. Situated between India and Tibet on the south side of this massive mountain chain, its numerous monasteries preserve an unbroken Tantric Buddhist tradition similar to that of the monasteries in Ladakh, Nepal and Sikkim.

The climate is humid and comparatively mild, and, during India's summer monsoon, it rains almost constantly. Elephants and tigers live in the southern part of the mountain jungles where screeching hordes of monkeys swing through the treetops. Huge ferns and bamboo forests line the roads. Wild orchids grow on vine-covered trees, and, during the spring months, entire forests of rhododendron and azaleas transform the landscape into an ocean of blossoms. The black bear still lives in the more elevated part of the country. If you are really lucky, you might encounter a white snow leopard high up near the Tibetan border.

More than half of the country is covered with these jungle-like mountain forests. The remaining fertile land is farmed by its modest and industrious inhabitants, the *drukpa*. Different dialects are spoken around the country, yet all students learn *dzongkha*, the language spoken and written in the monasteries. Goods are bartered at regularly scheduled Sunday markets, so little cash is needed. That might be the reason Bhutan is included in international statistics as one of the countries with the lowest per capita income, although the standard of living and quality of life are comparatively high. Hardly anybody lacks the basic necessities of life.

Until the end of the '60s, the country could only be crossed on foot, horse or yak. Every visitor had to show an invitation from the royal family. And although a road runs through the country today—probably one of the most winding roads in the world—you will hardly find more than a few dozen foreigners at a time in the "Land of the Dragons." Jigme Sengye Wangchuk, the young, wise King of Bhutan, protects his precious mountain country from uncontrolled streams of tourists. He has learned some lessons from the experiences of the neighboring countries. Just recently a law was passed to the effect that monasteries may only be visited by foreigners with special permission from the royal family.

Shabdong Ngawang Namgyal, who fled Tibet in the 17th century, is worshiped as the true founder of the Kingdom of Bhutan. Earlier he had been the head lama of the monastery of the Drukpa school (the Dragon Sect, in Ralung, Tibet). He was driven out by members of the "Yellow Hat" sect, the order to which the Dalai Lama belongs. This historical event explains the rather tense relationship between Bhutan and the "religious motherland," Tibet, as well as with the institution of the Dalai Lamas. Even today, Bhutan insists on the term "Himalayan Buddhism" to distinguish itself from "Tibetan Buddhism." The Bhutanese form of Buddhism belongs to the *Drukpa-Kagyupa* sect, a "Red Hat" school that has its roots in the unreformed "School of the Elders" (*Nyingmapa*). The Nyingmapa school was founded by the highly venerated Guru Padmasambhava, the "lotus-born one." He brought Buddhism from India via Tibet to Bhutan and other Himalayan countries.

36 • Wherever Tibetan culture is predominant, prayer flags flap in the wind. This image is from Drukyul, the "Land of the Dragons."

37 • More than half of the country is covered by mountain forests resembling jungles.

38 • Paro-Dzong in the kingdom of Bhutan. These imposing medieval fortresses are monasteries as well as administrative centers.

39 • *A novice (getsul) in Paro-Dzong. Until a few years ago, the monasteries were the only schools in Bhutan. Even today, social advancement is almost exclusively possible only through the monastic hierarchy.*

40 • In the "Land of the Dragons," as elsewhere, the population enthusiastically partakes in the big festivals of the monasteries, the main events of the year.

41 • In Paro-Dzong, a huge silk scroll painting (thangka) is unrolled once a year before sunrise and rolled back up when the first ray of sun appears. This tradition has been upheld for 300 years. The scroll depicts the highly venerated Padmasambhava (Guru Rinpoche), who brought Buddhism from Tibet to the "Land of the Dragons" in the 8th century.

42 • *According to legend, Padmasambhava, who was flying through the sky a tiger, landed here. This small mountain monastery therefore carries the name "tiger cave" (tagtsang).*

43 • *A peek through the mountainous jungle at the "far northern mountains" (a description already mentioned in ancient Greek texts). Legend has it that either the people in the mysterious country "beyond the source of the winds" were infinitely good, noble and wise—or that one-legged creatures with dog heads, who used ants as big as dogs to carry gold, lived there.*

44 • *The yak lives at high altitudes in Bhutan as well. It is sort of a symbol of all the strange conceptions people had formed from way back about this country, which, until a few years ago, was probably one of the most isolated in the world.*

45 • *In our thoughts we join the flight of the omnipresent shrieking crows and whistling mountain jackdaws as they sail across the Himalayas, the "Abode of the Snows," to the "Roof of the World."*

The mysterious country beyond the "Faraway Northern Mountains"

In their literary chronicles, even the ancient Greeks wondered about the people beyond the "Faraway Northern Mountains." And, indeed, Tibet has always been one of the least known and most inaccessible countries of the world. Small wonder then that Tibet has always provoked the most far-fetched and romantic notions in people's imagination.

Situated on the largest high-altitude plateau of our planet, Tibet is cut off from the Indian subcontinent by the immense Himalayan mountain range in the south. In the west the Karakoram is a natural bastion against invaders; in the north the country is protected by the Taklamakan Desert (an extension of the Gobi) and the Kunlun Mountains. In the northeast and east the dreaded Tsaidam marshes and the gorges and jagged mountains created by the upper reaches of the Yangtse, Mekong, Salween and Brahmaputra rivers make the journey to the Tibetan highland extremely difficult. The spectacular location, combined with a fervent desire for isolation on the part of the people and their government, helped create a unique culture that could not have survived anywhere else.

In spite of the difficulties, India, Nepal and China always maintained an economic and cultural exchange across the 16,500- to 20,000-foot-high passes. Thus the teachings of Lord Buddha found their way to the "Roof of the World" about one thousand years ago. These teachings changed the consciousness of the unrestrained and wild tribes. However, for centuries, hardly any outsiders have been able to stay long in the country with the exception of a few hardy missionaries and explorers (the latter sometimes disguised as monks).

Does the enigmatic and mythical country Shangri-La ("happy country") hold a message for us people of the 20th century? What is legend; what is truth? Today the door is open. Let us enter.

46 • The flight from Chengdu, the last border checkpoint in China, to Lhasa takes two hours. It gives us an open view of the immense mountains of Kham.

Central Tibet, Province U

This center of the sky,
this innermost part of the Earth,
this heart of the world,
fenced in by snow.
   —Anonymous, approx. 8th century

The flight from Chengdu to Lhasa

Finally, everything is ready for us to fly to the mysterious and legendary country that the inhabitants call *Bo-Yul*. Unknown and often unnamed majestic mountains reveal themselves to us through the plane's window as we fly through narrow valleys, because our Russian "turboprop" plane barely flies higher than 19,800 feet. Often the mountain peaks, covered by eternal snow and ice, jut into our air space, but the weather is clear, and the pilot is flying by sight.

We took off from Chengdu in Sichuan province and are now heading west towards the most inaccessible country on our planet. Beneath us lies the province of Kham, home of the Khampas, the tall, proud and warrior-like inhabitants of this mountain region.

The road built by the Chinese in the early '50s to enable them to link Tibet by force of arms to the "motherland" lies beneath us. Before the construction of the road, this ancient trade route between Tibet and China could only be traveled by caravans and took months. Even today, it takes military convoys ten to sixteen days, depending on weather and road conditions, to reach their military outpost in Tibet's capital. (They have to use nine out of ten of the fuel containers they are supposed to be bringing to the plateau for their own gas tanks just to get there!)

We, however, will be reaching the airfield near Lhasa in two-and-a-half hours. Modern times have caught up with Tibet. Could it be that the deities said to reside on these snow-covered peaks are amused by such thoughts?

The climate of Tibet

The poetic name for Tibet, "Abode of Snow," actually describes only the mountains surrounding the plateau. The plateau itself looks more like a high desert, similar to the area around Leh, Ladakh.

India's summer monsoon is held at bay by the Himalayan range. In the west the Karakoram blocks the mass of humid air, and in the north the dry and hot desert winds from the Tarim basin blow towards the plateau. The only humidity that Tibet receives comes from the northeast, from China, and this allows the nomads in Amdo to roam the land with their yak herds. Hardly any snow falls in the winter, which is why the passes up to approximately 20,000 feet are passable year-round.

Frequent sandstorms are a common nuisance; the sand comes through every crack, and you cannot really protect yourself against it. Short, violent thunderstorms accompanied by hail are also part of the rigors of the weather. Since the ground is not anchored by any type of vegetation, roads become impassable after a matter of minutes during such storms.

Lhasa lies on the same latitude as Cairo. However, because of its altitude, the radiation of the sun is unusually intense. The latest scientific research indicates that on the Tibetan plateau (with an average altitude of 15,800 feet) the solar energy per square meter can measure up to 1200 watts. Scientists suspect that the periodically recurring ice ages may be connected with this phenomenon.

47 • A view down the valley of the Tsangpo, called Brahmaputra in India, from an altitude of 19,800 feet. To the south the mass of humid air from India is building up. On its way up and across the highest mountain chain of the world, all this humidity will condense and come down as rain and snow on the mountains, leaving only dry winds to blow across Tibet.

"The Lake of the Upper Pastures," or turquoise lake as "big as a sixteen-day journey"

The turquoise Yamdok Lake glistens on the landscape like a jewel. Light and shadow play with the brown color of the high desert, and the surrounding mountains look as if they have been sprinkled with powdered sugar. Because of the intensity of the sun, this dusting of snow will have evaporated by noon, before ever melting into water.

I ask my Tibetan guide how large the lake is. After thinking for awhile his response is, "About sixteen days, I guess."

"Sixteen days," I reply. "What do you mean by that?"

"Sixteen days by horse," he answers. "By yak it would take twice as long."

Now I understand. In Tibet "horse days" or "yak days" are terms used for measuring distances. If you wanted to ride around the lake by horse, it would take sixteen days.

Even without being familiar with this measuring unit, I realize that this lake must be much bigger than the part that we can see from the 17,000-foot-high Karo-La pass.

This explains why older Tibetans living in exile in Switzerland sometimes do not know where they are on the planet. They know how far you can get in ten or even one hundred "horse days," so ten hours in a jet…that sounds like a good day's journey. Why then is their homeland supposed to be so far away?

48 • The turquoise-colored Yamdok Lake lies at an altitude of 13,850 feet and is embedded in a fascinating desert landscape.

Life in Tibet would be unthinkable without the yaks

The yak (*Poephagus grunniens*) is a subgenus of the aurochs. Wild yaks can still be found living in small numbers on top of the totally inhospitable Chang Tang plateau that lies at an altitude of 16,500 to 19,800 feet. The yak, with its huge coat of fur and "horse tail," is unusually strong yet also very undemanding. It is believed that mountain people domesticated the yak more than two thousand years ago. The Tibetans call the bull a *yak* and the female animal a *dri*. When a foreigner talks about "yak milk," the locals tend to ignore the mistake tactfully, with smiles on their faces.

In addition to *tsampa* (roasted barley flour), dairy products, especially the butter made from the rich dri milk, are the staple food of the Tibetans. Meat is reserved for holidays and taken dried on long treks. Their sturdy shoes are made out of the tanned skins, and the nomads weave the long hair of the yak tails into tents so durable that they can be passed on from generation to generation. The shorter belly hair is woven and sown into chubas, coat-like wraps. One yak can carry up to 220 pounds, even across snow and glaciers. Farmers harness these rather wild animals in front of their ploughs. And finally, yak dung is carefully collected, mostly by the children, and made into dried patties, an indispensable fuel substitute for wood, since wood is very rare in these mountainous regions.

49 • A farmer tilling his field with harnessed yaks. Because of the short growing season, the soil must not be ploughed too deeply.

How Buddhism came to the "Roof of the World"

Tibet's past history seems like an amalgam of legend and religion with history. According to legend, the first mythical kings descended from heaven in prehistoric times on a ribbon that also helped them find their way back to their celestial home after their deaths. Later a resentful minister supposedly cut the ribbon, turning the "graveless" kings into mortal kings.

What we know as history had its beginning only during the 7th century when the powerful King Songtsen Gampo (569-649) unified the country and introduced a written script. From then on, Tibet began leaving historical writings as we know them. One of his wives, the Chinese princess Wen-ch'ing, brought an enormous golden Buddha statue as part of her dowry to the inhospitable "Roof of the World." This statue depicting Prince Siddharta Gautama at the age of twelve is still the centerpiece of the Jo-khang hall in the Tsuglha-khang, the great "cathedral" of the holy city Lhasa. For many centuries this was the most venerated icon in the entire Himalayan region.

Songtsen Gampo built his first palace on a rocky knoll not far from this shrine, where the mighty Potala Palace stands today, and transformed the village "Rasa" (land of the goats) into the capital city of "Lhasa" (land of the Gods). Trade and cultural exchange with Nepal, India and China began to flourish. Buddhism, however, was initially mostly the religion for the court. The ordinary people adhered to their old shamanistic/animistic religion known today as "Bon."

By the 8th century, Tibet had become a great power. Tibetan troops penetrated deep into the Ganges delta, even captured the former Chinese capital Chang'an for a short period of time and occupied Samarkand, today part of Russia. The great magician Padmasambhava ("the lotus-born one") started building the first Buddhist monastery in Samyè, Tibet, together with the scholar Santarakshita ("maintained inner peace"). Under the reign of King Trisong Deutsen (755-797), it looked as if Buddhism would win over the old Bon religion.

But the dream of a Tibetan Empire and the hope that henceforth Buddhism would be able to spread freely came to an abrupt halt towards the middle of the 9th century, when Trisong Deutsen's grandson, Repatschen, was murdered by his brother, Prince Langdharma. Langdharma was an avid follower of the Bon religion and mercilessly and brutally persecuted everyone who took refuge in Buddhism. Langdharma, however, was killed in turn with an arrow by a Buddhist hermit disguised as a Bon dancer. Subsequently, Tibet was lost to history for two centuries as the empire fell apart and split up into several rival principalities. Buddhism seemed finally eradicated.

A first new ray of light appeared in 11th century with the arrival of the great Indian sage Atisha (982-1054). He represented the beginning of a teaching tradition that eventually, after the reform movement at the end of the 14th century, became part of the influential school of the "Yellow Hats," the order of the Dalai Lamas. However, the "Red Hat" sects, founded on the teachings of Padmasambhava, also gradually regrouped. Thus not only the Nyingmapa schools (the ancient tradition) gained new impetus but in addition new subgroups such as the Kagyupa and Sakyapa were founded in newly created monasteries all over the country. Two hundred years later these were to become politically very influential.

A summary of the history of Tibet up to the reformation would be incomplete without mentioning the name of the ascetic hermit Milarepa (the "cotton-clad one"), who lived from 1040 to 1123. He was a great sage and gifted poet who is said to have written one hundred thousand verses. Since he was a layman and did not belong to a monastic order, he felt free to bitterly criticize the disintegration of manners and morals in certain monasteries at the beginning of the 12th century. At one point the "cotton-clad one" wrote the following to unrestrained monks: "Your bellies are bursting with pride and arrogance; you are burping up vanity and vomiting jealousy!" Although the exhortations of the hermit did not fall entirely on deaf ears, the moral disintegration of the monasteries could be stopped only two hundred years later by the great reformer Tsongkhapa, who was known by his nickname as the "man from the onion valley." He created the order of the "virtuous ones" and, between 1409 and 1419, founded the three great state monasteries: Ganden ("filled with joy"), Drepung ("heap of rice") and Sera ("grove of wild roses"), all in the vicinity of Lhasa.

The reformation was facilitated by the improvement in printing techniques and the fact that, in the meantime, all the Buddhist scriptures had been translated into Tibetan. From a historical/cultural point of view, this represented a colossal achievement. The Kanjur, the translation of the words of Buddha, contains 108 volumes, and the Tanjur, the later commentaries, contains 225 expansive folios. According to Tibetans, it would require a caravan of thirty yaks to transport all the holy scriptures of a monastery.

During the 13th century, a political development of far-reaching consequences was initiated between the powerful head lamas of the Sakya monasteries and the rulers of the Mongolian Empire. Still today, the Chinese base their claims on Tibet on this political development. The powerful Mongolian prince Godan, the son of Ugedai and grandson of Gengis Khan, sent a cordial, yet not to be ignored invitation to the Head Lama of the Sakyas to visit his state. Understanding this to be a command performance, the high lama sent his 10-year-old nephew, Pagpa Lodro Gyaltsen, ahead as a pledge while he allowed himself more than two years to travel to Lake Kokonor. However, by the time his uncle arrived, the little lama had already won over the hearts of everybody around him with his charm and precocious intellect to the extent that half of the court was already open to the peaceable Buddhist doctrine. Subsequently, a kind of "Emperor-Pope" relationship developed between the Sakya Pandita and the powerful Prince Godan. From that time on, the Mongolians could consider themselves the temporal rulers of Tibet, while the Tibetans represented the spiritual power. The little Pagpa attained fame and glory at the court of the Mongolian prince and was proclaimed viceroy of Tibet, while the Sakya monastery became the religious and administrative center of Tibet.

50 • View of the fabulous "Potala." Is it a palace? A fortress? A monastery? Built by the "Great Fifth" in the 17th century, this monumental building has been the seat of the Tibetan "god-kings," the Dalai Lamas, without interruption until 1959 and is without a doubt one of the largest and most impressive structures on earth.

51 • While the Potala is now a museum, religious life is being revived in other monasteries on a modest scale. But the learned high lamas, the initiated masters, are no longer there. In the long run, the religion cannot survive without them. They either were killed during the Chinese Cultural Revolution or fled to India. From there, some of them have found their way to the Western world, where they are now working as spiritual teachers.

The Tradition of the Dalai Lamas

And so it came about that the Venerable Lama Sonam Gyatso received the honorary title of "Dalai Lama" in 1578 from the Mongolian ruler Altan Khan. "Dalai" is Mongolian and means "ocean of the world," whereas "Lama" is Tibetan and means "superior." He is said to be the third Dalai Lama in Tibetan history; two of his predecessors were proclaimed the first and second Dalai Lamas posthumously. Thus, a unique tradition was born with Sonam Gyatso. The title "Dalai Lama" is not hereditary since the Gelugpa monks live in strict celibacy. Nor can it be bestowed. The tradition is founded on the belief, normal for every Buddhist, that human beings will reincarnate in another existence on earth after their death. In the tradition of the Dalai Lamas the bearer of this highest title has to be rediscovered after he has left his old body and reincarnated in that of a small child. It would go beyond the scope of our brief summary of the history of Tibet to talk in detail about the trials and tribulations of the fourteen "god-kings." We might only mention Lobsang Gyatso, who went down in history as the "Great Fifth." He lived from 1617 until 1682 and built the mighty Potala Palace such as it still exists today. He was also the Dalai Lama who, together with his teacher Lobsang Chogyi Gyeltsen, founded the second great incarnation lineage, that of the Panchen Lamas. More about the present, 14th Dalai Lama, Tenzin Gyatso, who is living in exile in India today, in a later chapter.

52 • View of the Potala Palace from the roof of Tibet's most sacred shrine, the "Jo-khang." The latter is part of the temple complex known as "Tsuglhakang." Thousands of pious pilgrims circumambulate the temple via the "Barkhor" road every day in a clockwise direction.

53 • *Jowo Rinpoche is
the most venerated icon
of the entire Himalayan
region. This statue that
almost disappears
under the weight of its
ornaments was brought
to Lhasa in the 7th
century by the Chinese
princess Wen-ch'ing as
part of her dowry.*

54 • *Praying pilgrims
in front of the
Jo-khang temple, the
so-called "Lhasa
Cathedral." It is the
fervent wish of every
Tibetan to pay
reverence to Jowo
Rinpoche, an
emanation of the
Buddha, at least once
in a lifetime, even if it
means making an
arduous journey of
weeks or even months.*

55 • A pilgrim is continuously turning a prayer wheel to keep the "teachings" flowing, another form of meditation. The 108 beads of her rosary are gliding through her fingers while she recites "om mani padme hum, om mani padme hum…" Although she is unable to read the holy scriptures, she feels totally in tune with her religion.

56 • Today the traditional clothing is worn mostly by older people. A woman is entering a shrine housing an enormous prayer wheel. She will hold on to the railing with her right hand and, walking in a clockwise direction, set the wheel in motion. The religious content of the wheel is thus kept in motion, which is considered to be a commendable act. Isn't motion life—and life sacred?

The "Golden Rooftops of Lhasa"

The great Tibetan monasteries always had an almost mythical reputation because of their golden rooftops. Below we see not the "golden rooftops of Lhasa," but those of the monastery of Tashi-Lhunpo near Shigatse. Thanks to small offerings made by innumerable devotees over centuries, the gold shines and sparkles in the sunlight and lets the heart of the devout visitor beat faster. What a thrill it must be for the pilgrims to look down from the last mountain pass onto this golden splendor in the valley after a long journey full of deprivation!

We people in the West have more and more forgotten how to enjoy such communal riches. We believe that something has to "belong" to us in order to make us happy. Also, some visitors to Tibet are shocked to see the wealth of the monasteries on the one hand, and the poverty of the population on the other. But wouldn't the "distribution of the riches amongst the needy," which seems to us the fair thing, be exactly the opposite of what has been happening here for many centuries: i.e. the collecting of small and even tiny offerings to realize a great project for the entire community? Be that as it may, these treasures belong to all who enjoy them.

57 • The golden rooftops of the monastery Tashi-Lhunpo in Shigatse. This magnificent monastic complex has been the seat of the Panchen Lamas, the second-highest reincarnation lineage of the country, since the 17th century.

58 • Prayer flags
flapping in the wind,
as well as the
charming decorations
on yak tails, always
come in the symbolic
colors: red, blue, green,
yellow—and white,
the "color" that
mysteriously combines
all other colors within
it and therefore
symbolizes their origin.

59 • *Riding competitions have always been part of the pleasures of all peoples of the Asian steppes. Yet yak races are rare, even in Tibet, the land of the yaks. Here, one of these spectacular events is taking place outside the gates of the rebuilt Samyè monastery. Spurred on by the crowd, the daring riders are screaming wildly while galloping towards the goal on these huge beasts.*

60 • *The rider on the bucking yak bull reminds one of a cowboy breaking in a young horse.*

61 • Since Tibet is cold and has very little water, the diaper problem is solved very simply.

Tibetans and hygiene

Tibetans are not obsessed with what we consider physical hygiene. According to our Western standards, everything is basically dirty. In Tibet, because of the climatic conditions in winter, the unheated houses and tents, personal hygiene in the Western sense would be impossible. Besides, soap dries out the skin and is therefore considered to be damaging in this extremely dry climate. This aversion towards washing is reflected in the attitude of the nomads, who consider a young girl trying to wash her face as quite vain. Instead, they like to rub (usually rancid) butter on their hands and face as a kind of cosmetic care. This smell combines with the smoke of the constantly burning yak dung fires and body odors to create, over time, the unique and distinctive "perfume" that is familiar to all visitors to Tibet.

62 • Tibetan children are not shy in front of a camera. On the contrary, they love to pose whenever given a chance and exude a very natural charm.

The country where children are king

In all the Buddhist regions of the Himalayas children are taken more seriously than perhaps anywhere else in the world. Because of the Buddhist belief in reincarnation the child is seen as a complete human personality that simply still has an incomplete body in the first years of its earthly existence, and requires special care, just like a growing plant. Because of this attitude, the small "god-kings" are treated with the greatest respect, although their upbringing is strict. The priest-king Sakya Pandita, whose grandson won over the Mongolian court to Buddhism with his charm and wisdom, said: "If it is good advice, one should listen to the words of a child."

Is it not often the case that children teach us lessons instead of the other way around? Their openness, honesty and directness can embarrass us at times.

The philosopher Walter Robert Corti said the following on the occasion of the inauguration of the Tibetan House in the Pestalozzi Children's Village in Switzerland: "Children are the last human tribe left to be discovered on our planet, one without a legislation or king, without a parliament or an army. For thousands of years it has been living right among us, probably without ever having achieved a sense of self-awareness, but on its small feet the human family as a whole moves forward."

Whether they live as nomads on the Tibetan plateau or grow up in New York skyscrapers, whether they are born in an Inuit igloo or live in the slums of an Indian city, children all have one thing in common: they still speak the language of the heart.

Let's reflect on the history of nations: Isn't it full of malice, striving for power, envy, prejudice and the most hideous cruelty? This is true of all nations—including Tibet. But are the children to blame?

What causes this tribe of hopeful, radiant children to become Chinese or Tibetans, Muslims or Hindus, Gelugpas, Kagyupas or Sakyapas? Can there still be any hope that the human race will one day decide in favor of humanity? We adults are the ones who poison these children with our ideas, prejudices, dogmas and laws until they gradually forget the language of children and no longer understand themselves and others; then they turn against each other—and finally fight each other until the last breath...

Gautama Buddha preached a doctrine that has the purity of a child and is infinitely tolerant. And Jesus Christ warned us: "Except ye become as little children ye shall not enter into the Kingdom of Heaven." If only one day there could be a country in which the children are kings, and the kings are as pure of heart as children...

63 • *A boy outside the wall of the Sakya monastery. Sometimes ancient human souls seem to shine through the serious faces of these children.*

The Former Province of Amdo in Northeastern Tibet

64 • *The Amnyè Machen Pomra, the holy mountain of the marauding Golog nomads, was for a long time, even in the West, considered the tallest mountain in the world, although it had not been measured. Since 1982 we know that it is "only" 20,730 feet high. The mountain deity Machen Pomra is depicted as a warrior-god on a pale horse that is as fast as the wind.*

The holy mountain Amnyè Machen

Out of the far northeastern corner of the Tibetan plateau, in the former Tibetan province of Amdo, rises the mountain Amnyè Machen, which is considered a sacred mountain by the Golog nomads. It is the first and also the highest elevation of the Kunlun range that stretches along the entire northern border of ethnic Tibet and ends in the west with the Pamirs. The wild torrents that spring from its glaciers feed the headwaters of the famous "Yellow River." In the north, at an elevation of 10,560 feet, lies the largest steppe lake of the world, the Kokonor or "Blue Lake." A few hundred kilometers to the northeast of the holy mountain lies one of the most important monastic cities of Tibet, Kumbum. It was built at the birthplace of the great reformer Tsongkhapa. Nearby is the village of Taktser, the birthplace of the present 14th Dalai Lama.

The Amnyè Machen massif has three main peaks: the southernmost is called Chenrezig, the middle one Amnyè Machen, and the northern and highest one Dradul Lungchag. The middle peak, from which the entire mountain takes its name, is said to be inhabited by the deity Machen Pomra. Up to ten thousand Tibetans a year used to circumambulate the mountain on foot, along a well-worn path.

From a linguistic point of view the meaning of the name Amnyè Machen is not totally clear. According to folk etymology, one could deduce that *mat-chin* means "Great Mother." The two Tibetan syllables sound like "Mother" and "great," but they are spelled differently. The name probably means the great "Peacock Ancestor." Since "Amnyè" is an honorary title, "Amnyè Machen" could be translated as "The Venerable Peacock Mountain." The so-called

"Yellow River" also carries the syllable "ma" (*Machu*) in its name and therefore means "Peacock Water" or "Peacock River." In the Brockhaus encyclopedia (1966, Wiesbaden) the following can be read under the headword Amnyè Matchin: "Holy mountain in the great loop of the Upper Hoangho in the Jischi-Chan, a mountain chain of the Kunlun system. It was said to be 9,000 meters (29,700 feet) high but a Chinese expedition in 1960 reported a height of 7160 meters (23,600 feet)."

The confusion regarding the height of Amnyè Machen started in 1922. The British General Pereira, who had been trying to find a route to Lhasa, mentioned to Joseph F. Rock, an American botanist and geographer, that Amnyè Machen might be the highest mountain in the world. When Pereira died shortly thereafter, Rock took it upon himself to further investigate this suggestion. He risked his life by getting within fifty miles of the mountain, as the wild Gologs did not allow any outsiders on their land. Boiling water to determine at which altitude he was, and measuring the mountain with the help of a theodolite, Rock decided that its height was 29,700 feet. He was able to publish this discovery in the respected magazine *National Geographic*, although the editors cautiously reduced the number to 28,000 feet.

In 1944 a press release went around the world. The crew of an American DC-3 went off-course and supposedly saw the mountain. Later on it was decided that the report had been a joke. How could a propeller-driven airplane from the '30s have flown that far and especially that high!

When Leonard Clark, a former CIA officer, made his way through the dreaded Golog region with a heavily armed expedition and got within fifteen miles of the mountain, suspense built up among the experts. The measurement then resulted in 29,661 feet, which would have made it the highest mountain in the world!

After his exciting discovery had been published in *Life Magazine* and Clark had written about the details in his book *The Marching Wind*, the legend was complete. Then, in 1960, yet another expedition came back from Amnyè Machen with the sobering report that the peak was only 23,491 feet high. However, at the beginning of the '70s, it became known that not only had the expedition climbed the wrong summit but the measurement had been wrong as well. Thus the holy mountain Amnyè Machen had to wait until 1980 when it was "conquered" by a Japanese expedition. Today its height is acknowledged to be 20,730 feet. Is this its real height or only the latest in a series of mistakes? The mountain itself and its worshipers, the Golog, could hardly care less.

65 • *This proud chief of the Golog bandits, who halted our convoy, inspires respect.*

The nomadic tribe of the Gologs

From the perspective of the Chinese, the region that is inhabited by the Golog is the "Wild West." If you believe the reports of travelers, even contemporary ones, this nomadic tribe of bandits was truly the terror of all the peaceful nomads and posed the greatest threat to travelers.

Accompanied by women and children, they would go all the way up to the Tsaidam marshes in search of loot and behave like the notorious hordes of Genghis Khan. Rumor has it that, in order to instill terror, they used to have the heads of their dead enemies dangling from their saddles by the hair. Even if we take into account that Orientals love to spin yarns and grossly exaggerate, there is still enough indescribable cruelty left in their stories, which we do not want to go into here. These wild hordes were under the command of an equally wild tribal princess, the legendary Chimi Dolma. The German explorer Ernst Schafer reported in 1935 that she had seventeen husbands and seven thousand bodyguards who accompanied her once a year to the Amnyè Machen for the circumambulation of the sacred mountain on horseback. According to legend, she is said to have climbed the mountain nude every year to meditate on the deity. In 1939, Chimi Dolma was executed by a Chinese punitive expedition.

66 • This tribe of Golog nomads is in charge of seven hundred yaks which graze on seven hundred square kilometers of land. "Keep the dogs back" is the greeting you have to yell from a safe distance before you approach a nomad's tent. Only once the wild, aggressive guard dogs are tied up can you assume that you are welcome to visit. If not, the answer is "stay away, foreigner."

67 • The rainbow-colored border on the "chuba" of this proud woman shows that she belongs to the tribe of the Golog bandits. She dressed herself and her daughter up, because a neighboring family had announced their visit. The silver case (gau) around her neck contains an amulet and prayers.

68 • 108 braids
decorate the head of
this child (because the
"kanjur," the teachings
of Lord Buddha, is said
to have contained 108
volumes), 108 being a
sacred number to
Tibetans.

In sharp contrast to these intimidating stories, we came to know the good side of these people while traveling through their territory. The men leading the yaks and horses on the way to the base camp of the holy mountain were taciturn and sullen; they seemed to consider their services as "guides" to be far beneath their dignity. But when we were finally invited into a nomad tent after many futile attempts, we did get a sense of what it means to be a guest of the Gologs. We were offered butter tea and tsampa, and, since our Chinese companion did not dare to enter the tent, we were even proudly shown the house altar. This was still quite risky in the fall of 1983. I even dared to take some photographs inside the tent, although I must admit that my heart was beating wildly when I focused on the little son and heir lying in a pile of sheep skins and the flash went off. Upon leaving, the owner of the tent accompanied us part of the way. When we wanted to give him a gift, a Swiss watch, he proudly refused it. Hospitality is sacred to them and no gift is expected in return.

69 • These two shepherd girls are very shy about coming into the tent, because it is the first time that "white long noses" are their guests.

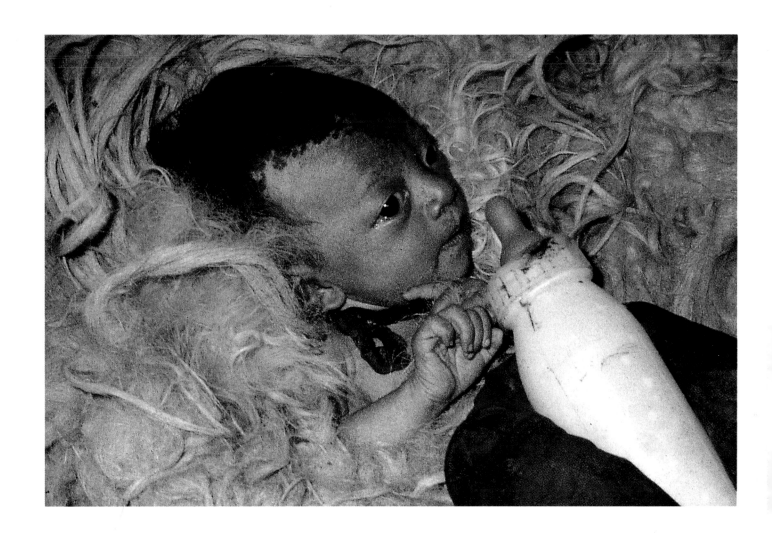

70 • *In the very back of the tent, the black eyes of the future bandit chief look out from a huge pile of sheepskins.*

The Suffering of a People
Flight and Exile

71 • *"Destroy the old, create the new!" was the devastating battle cry of the "Red Guards" who raged and pillaged in Tibet during the Cultural Revolution. Thousands of monastic complexes such as the state monastery of Ganden were so badly destroyed that only the foundations were left. A few of the buildings like the red mausoleum of the reformer Tsongkhapa have been rebuilt in recent years.*

72 • *"Watch the fire, do not keep the ashes." This is the only maxim that will help the advanced Tibetan culture and religion survive in exile.*

The destroyed monastic complex of Ganden—a shameful memorial

This photograph of the once splendid monastic city of Ganden—now a pile of rubble except for a few recently restored buildings—is a reminder of the reign of terror known as the Chinese "Cultural Revolution" that was unleashed between 1965 and 1975 in the highlands of Tibet. It is a pathetic memorial to human ignorance. In deep consternation we are forced to realize what unspeakable suffering man causes to his fellow men when allowed to be driven by desire and hatred due to profound ignorance. The destruction of thousands of monasteries and places of worship in Tibet is final and can never be atoned for. The Chinese people, who pride themselves on having a highly developed culture that has endured for thousands of years, have committed a shameful deed that cannot be swept away by any reform programs, however liberal, nor by the partial reconstruction of the monasteries and temples. "Destroy the old, create the new!" was the battle cry of the—mostly young—people who were led astray by the paramilitary "Red Guards." But who today is willing to take responsibility for having led these people astray? To quote an old saying among students: "Tradition means tend to the fire but do not keep the ashes." The Tibetan monasteries have been reduced to rubble and ashes, but their spirit is unbroken.

73 • Norbulinka, the "Garden of Jewels," was the summer palace of the Dalai Lama. On March 17, 1959, Tenzin Gyatso, the 14th Dalai Lama, was compelled to flee his country from here. During the ensuing months, approximately one hundred thousand Tibetans followed him into exile in India and other Himalayan countries. Now they are tending the "fire" in exile, and the teachings have reached the "red-cheeked people," fulfilling the ancient prophesy of Padmasambhava.

The prophecy of Padmasambhava is being fulfilled

The vision of the great tantric master Padmasambhava, according to which "the man from the land of snow" must leave his country "when the time comes that iron birds can fly and horses roll on wheels" began to become a historical reality in the early '50s. The non-violent liberation of the Indian subcontinent from the British colonial power by Mahatma Gandhi created a kind of power vacuum in the region between China, Russia and India. Thus, the troops of Mao Tsetung, who only shortly before had assumed power in China, took advantage of the favorable situation and invaded Tibet. Their designs focused on the strategic location of Tibet and its abundance of mineral resources.

The occupation of Tibet was justified to the general public as a "fight against feudalism and slavery." Even though the 1914 Treaty of Simla, drafted to legally settle the borders between Tibet and neighboring states, was not signed by the Chinese, it is indisputable that Tibet, during the reign of the 13th Dalai Lama, used the fall of the last Chinese imperial dynasty at the beginning of the century to free itself from its powerful neighbor and declare its independence.

Shortly after the first Chinese troops marched into Lhasa in 1951, the then only 15-year-old 14th Dalai Lama was given full authority of the state, which had been shared by his two regents, Reting Rinpoche and Tagdra Rinpoche, during his childhood. The first few years of the young god-king's reign were characterized by his will to execute reforms and find a peaceful solution with Peking through diplomacy. A seventeen-point agreement was drawn up in which China guaranteed the Tibetans cultural and religious autonomy under Chinese sovereignty. But the political atmosphere grew darker and darker. Not only were the provisions of the agreement treated with contempt by the Chinese, the world at large was unaware—or did not want to acknowledge for political reasons—the tragedy that was looming over Tibet. On March 10, 1959, the floodgates of repressed hatred and anger towards the unpopular "liberators" opened and a chapter of unspeakable suffering in the history of Tibet began. The spark that triggered the explosion was an invitation by the Chinese military authorities to the young god-king. He was supposed to visit a theater performance in Lhasa without taking along any personal escorts. Such, at least, was the rumor that spread among the people. The inhabitants of Lhasa, who feared for his life, formed a human wall around the summer palace where His Holiness was residing. They wanted to protect him and, at the same time, avoid the rash acceptance of the invitation. After several appeals to Tenzin Gyatso to comply with the invitation were ignored, the Chinese military began shelling the palace. However, unbeknownst to them, the 14th Dalai Lama had secretly left his residence at nightfall with a small entourage and was already heading south. His plan was to wait in southern Tibet and see how things developed, as he had done once before, in 1951. But Chinese air attacks and ground commandos forced him to continue and make the long, terribly exhausting trek across the border into India. According to the Tibetans, approximately two hundred thousand people were killed during the bloody upheaval; eighty thousand fled to the neighboring countries of India, Nepal, Sikkim and Bhutan, one thousand refugees were eventually invited to settle in Switzerland and two hundred were brought to Canada by the Canadian government.

74 • *An Indian monk says his morning prayer on the holy river Ganges, near Sarnath in India. The Buddha's teachings originated near here some 2500 years ago.*

75 • His Holiness, the
14th Dalai Lama,
praying in
Dharamsala, his
Indian residence-in-
exile, for the well-being
of his countrymen and
for world peace.

76 • *The monks of the reformed school, the sect to which the Dalai Lama belongs, are called "Yellow Hats" (Gelugpas) because of the color of their ceremonial hats.*

77 • *All the monks of the different sects or schools of Tibetan Buddhism wear maroon-colored robes.*

78 • *Reverence and deep devotion are reflected in the face of this monk. To be in the presence of Yeshe Norbu ("Jewel of Wisdom"), as Tibetans call the Dalai Lama, is a priceless gift for them.*

The Tibetan culture in exile

During the 11th and 12th centuries, Muslim invaders attacked northern India from Afghanistan and almost totally destroyed the Buddhist monasteries and universities. Many monks were driven away or killed, others fled into the northern mountains and, eventually, Tibet became a place of refuge for Indian Buddhism. With the occupation of Tibet by the Chinese in 1950 and the atrocities committed by the Red Guards, the tragedy repeated itself. Now, almost a thousand years after the Muslim invasion, India has again become a place of refuge for Buddhism—this time the Tibetan form of Mahayana Buddhism—where the monastic culture of Tibet is being kept alive. In the course of the last thirty years, monasteries and monastic schools of the different traditions have been reestablished all across India. Today there are probably more than fifty altogether. Even the huge state monasteries were reestablished in exile in the south Indian state of Karnataka—Ganden and Drepung near Mundgod and the famous monastic university of Sera in Bylakuppe, east of Mysore. The Dalai Lama's residence-in-exile is situated in the foothills of the Himalayas, in McLeod Ganj, above the town of Dharamsala in the northern Indian state of Himachal Pradesh. It is from here that His Holiness looks after his people in India and the rest of the world. Today, well over one hundred thousand Tibetans are living in India and the kingdom of Nepal, about two thousand have found a new home in Switzerland, and several thousand have emigrated to other countries in Europe or to the USA and Canada.

79 • The teachings are starting to reach the "red-cheeked men," just as the great master Padmasambhava predicted in the 8th century. Here a young Western monk is lighting a butter lamp.

As a result of the resettling of Tibetan refugees, Buddhism made its way to the Western countries. It would be beyond the scope of this publication to investigate the question why it took almost two thousand years for the Christian Western world to take notice of the tolerant, peace-loving teachings of Buddhism that focus on compassion. Is it possible that the Islamic faith played the role of a bolt between the Christian and Buddhist cultures? It is quite likely that the "enemy concept" that Christianity constructed around Islam as a religion in direct competition with it was unconsciously projected onto all the other earlier religions whose devotees were not baptized and therefore considered to be "pagans." All the same, today Buddhism has penetrated our rigid religious thinking. The West is willing to realize that Buddhist philosophy does not actually contradict that of any other religion. Realization is not a question of belief, but rather of direct insight. Things that separate are to be found at all times and everywhere. Let us keep a lookout for the things that connect us. Ultimately, there is only one truth.

The Tibetan refugees did not arrive empty-handed

As a result of their forced exodus, the Tibetan refugees have brought us a gift in the form of a highly advanced culture and religion preserved from ancient times. The Tibetan form of Buddhism has especially aroused great interest among experts and lay practitioners in Western countries. With the refugees arrived many highly-attained lamas who are now giving teachings in Europe and the Americas and are helping us understand the hitherto secret and encoded holy scriptures, some of which date back more than a thousand years.

This is of priceless value not only for us Westerners but also for Tibetans in exile. The old traditions are their support in the Western diaspora and provide them with a strong feeling of solidarity. The interest that people in the West have taken in their culture is reinforcing their self-esteem and supporting the way they see themselves. Besides that, the Dalai Lama is a very unifying figure for them. Without him, these mountain people might quickly split up again into different ethnic minorities such as the Khampas and Amdowas, or people from U and Tsang, a danger that had existed in old Tibet.

81 • The late Ven. Kalu Rinpoche of the Kagyu school of Tibetan Buddhism during a Buddhist initiation in Stockholm, Sweden.

82 • *A highly-attained master from the Himalayas, the Ven. Song Rinpoche, is elucidating the doctrine for his countrymen in exile.*

83 • *In Rikon, Switzerland, the different classical traditions of Tibetan Buddhism were unified under the same roof for the first time in the long history of Tibetan Buddhism. In this photograph the Ven. Sakya Trinzin, the head of the Sakyapa order, is giving a teaching.*

The purpose and activities of the Tibetan Monastic Institute in Switzerland

Thanks to a private initiative, more than 150 Tibetan children found new homes with Swiss families in the early '60s. From 1961 onwards, on the invitation of the Swiss people and under the patronage of the Swiss Red Cross, other Tibetan refugees started arriving. Today, more Tibetans are living in Switzerland than in any other country in the Western Hemisphere.

Very early on, it became clear that it was not enough to only take care of the physical well-being of the resettled Tibetans. A life without religion was practically inconceivable for these Buddhist immigrants. Our most pressing task was to create a center for Tibetan Buddhist culture and religion. Thus, thanks to a private initiative, a *gompa,* or Tibetan monastery and academic institute, was founded in Rikon, near Zurich. The monastic community, initially consisting of only an abbot and five monks, took over the task of looking after the cultural and spiritual needs of their countrymen and giving them teachings. Since then, the Tibetan Institute affiliated with the monastery has been in the service of the general public and, to quote the institute's guidelines, is supporting "academic research in the fields of history of religion, literature, music and art history as well as in the fields of linguistics, medicine and pharmacology." From a general point of view, the goal of the Tibetan Institute is to facilitate a meeting between Tibetan and Western cultures.

84 • The Tibetan letters "Cho-Khor-Gon" are inscribed above the entrance of the monastery in Rikon near Zurich and stand for "Monastery of the Wheel of the Dharma." The eight spokes of the wheel symbolize the "eight-fold path," the message of the first teachings of Lord Buddha in the Deer Park at Sarnath in India.

85 • The Tibetan Monastic Institute in Rikon, Switzerland, where Tibetan prayer flags have been flying in the wind since 1968. While the monastic community is looking after their countrymen in exile, the institute is also open to Western seekers and scholars interested in Buddhism.

Everyday life in the monastery in Rikon

The daily life of the monk community in Rikon starts between seven and eight o'clock with group morning prayer in the shrine room of the monastery. After breakfast, the lamas retreat to their cells to study the scriptures and do their personal worship and meditation. The rest of the morning is reserved for academic work, translations and similar activities.

After a simple lunch, the monks dedicate their time to the spiritual welfare and education of their fellow Tibetans. Contrary to the traditional Tibetan ways, these monks do not always stay in the monastery, but also practice active spiritual welfare by visiting the families and educating the children and youths in their homes. The cultural highlights are the big and small festivities connected with the religious Tibetan Buddhist holidays. Dressed in traditional clothes, most Tibetans take part in the festive *pujas*.

From time to time the monastery accommodates high-ranking Tibetan lamas living in exile in India, who are traveling in Europe. These lamas often take the opportunity to give teachings here. Every Tibetan considers it a great blessing when, every few years, His Holiness the Dalai Lama comes to stay on the upper floor of the monastery to give interviews and to talk to the community.

86 • The novice Lobsang Tempa lighting a butter lamp in the shrine room of the Tibetan Monastic Institute in Rikon.

87 • Geshe Khedup
performing a fire puja
with a lay devotee
from Rikon.

The Kalachakra initiation

During the Kalachakra initiation, which, in old Tibet, a Dalai Lama performed only a few times during his lifetime, the participants are initiated into the great mystery of "time and space." This is the most important initiation known to Tibetan Buddhists and is performed during a ceremony lasting from new moon to full moon. *Kala* means "time," *chakra*, "wheel."

The aim of every initiation is to acquaint us with something unknown, something "mysterious." These kinds of initiations (in Latin: *inire*, "to enter") are usually accompanied by sacred symbolic rites for which certain requirements are necessary and commitments are involved. The person wishing to be initiated needs to fulfill the necessary requirements for the initiation and be willing to responsibly carry the power arising from the newly acquired knowledge. This type of knowledge transmission cannot be achieved without outside help; it is performed by an already initiated master, a mystic.

These are the prerequisites for an initiation. But the question concerning the "mystery" itself is not yet answered.

The mystery of all mysteries is that, in reality, there is no mystery. The moment we have the answer, there no longer is a mystery! For a child who has not yet learned to read and write, the characters are a deep mystery, and yet for everyone who can read these lines, the "mystery" has been revealed. We have all once been initiated by a school "master" into the secret—how black signs need to be arranged on a white surface, so that a third party can read our thoughts by looking at them. We call that writing and reading. Did we not acquire great power as well as responsibility in this way?

During an important initiation, death and rebirth are often talked about. Yes indeed, the illiterate has died and a person knowing how to read and write is born. Initiations are transits leading to an expansion of consciousness, steps or stages on the way to the goal. But where do these stages lead us? The question remains: "Who am I?" It only makes sense to ask about the goal, if we want to find out who it is, who is searching. This is why, in the third part of this book, we will go in search of ourselves with the help of the Buddhist philosophy…we will go on an inner journey.

88 • In July, 1985, an initiation took place in a tented camp close to Tibetan Monastic Institute of Rikon in Switzerland, in which more than six thousand Tibetans, Western Buddhists and lay people from thirty-seven countries took part.

89 • On a quiet and clear full-moon night, the Dalai Lama initiated the participants into the innermost mystery of the Kalachakra mandala.

90 • *Four monks from Namgyal Monastery are drawing the Kalachakra mandala with colored sand. For seven days they worked in utter concentration on this breathtakingly beautiful and intricate design of the Kalachakra "Wheel of Time."*

91 • *The fine, colored sand is in the tapered tube. With a second tool the monks gently rub along the serrated upper surface of the tube, causing the vibrations to let the sand trickle out of the point in a fine stream.*

92 • "Whatever was conditionally created must die again; everything is empty in its essence," according to the Buddhist doctrine. Thus, at the end of the initiation the mandala is swept into a silver vessel and scattered into the waters of the little river Toss, together with flowers and other offerings.

The Buddhist Path of
Realization
An Inner Journey

A dialogue between East and West

"East is East and West is West, and never the twain shall meet," wrote the author Rudyard Kipling at the beginning of this century. And it is true that East and West were absolute polar opposites in the past.

The East was the cradle of the great mystical world religions. Human beings were looking for the path to their inner being and a way to attain the inner strength of "nonattachment." The people of the Orient were striving for liberation from the forever repeating cycle of existence (*samsara*). They recognized that the craving for worldly things and attainments is the root cause of all suffering. What was demanded was not blind faith but insight, not knowledge but wisdom. Due to their passive, humble attitude Eastern people were always willing to give in to the circumstances, to "surrender."

The West, on the other hand, tried already at the time of Alexander the Great to subjugate the world. Western man wanted to dominate not only foreign nations but also nature and its laws. Even God was to be conquered! Western man has always strived for wealth and power, and his ambitious goal is to acquire ever more possessions. These active efforts did bring about material results—he can fly to the moon and has the capacity to unleash gigantic destructive forces, because he has discovered the secret of the laws of matter and energy.

A person in the East may live at peace with himself yet has never learned how to free himself from poverty, misery and illness; his counterpart in the West has lost the path to his innermost self despite his material prosperity. He is desperately searching for the meaning and purpose of his existence and is deeply disappointed that, despite everything, he is unable to find what he really hopes for most, true happiness in life.

Many young people in Western countries and, even more so, spiritually oriented as well as advanced scientists are finally realizing that we cannot continue on this path, that this craving for more and more possessions is destroying the world. And thus a new way of thinking has taken root. Slowly the realization is gaining ground that we are living a life of spiritual poverty and disorientation despite our material prosperity and that we are therefore unable to master our problems in life. For years now, a search for the true spiritual values has been taking place. As a result, many have discovered the eternal truths of the wise teachings of the East.

As we shall see, unlike almost all other religions, Buddhism is not a declaration of faith but a path to realization. And realization is also the path of the natural sciences. Realization is the first big bridge towards an understanding between East and West!

The two great religious currents of humanity

Among the five great world religions we generally include Judaism, Christianity and Islam in the West, Hinduism and Buddhism in the East. Yet, basically, there are but two religious currents of humanity, as the three religions of the West all have their roots in the Old Testament of Abraham and could be called "Abrahamic religions" (if there were such a term).

The two great religions of the East, Hinduism and Buddhism, are based on what are probably the most ancient scriptures of humanity, the *Vedas*. Their origin can be traced back to

1500 B.C., although the oral tradition is surely much older. In the days of Gautama Buddha, the most essential parts of this gigantic work were complete. It was written in Sanskrit, the classical language of India. During the 9th century A.D., its contents were reexamined by the Hindu reformer Shankaracharya and joined together as a seamless conception of the world which we today call the philosophy of Vedanta.

A verse from that time reads:

All teachings ultimately lead to the highest reality;
Pilgrims head towards the same city at different speeds,
From different points of departure and at different times.

The concept of time in East and West

The famous Indologist from Tubingen, Professor Helmuth von Glasenapp, used to say to his students: "West of the Hindukush time is running; east of it time stands still." In the West we believe that time is constantly running and that we have to think in terms of our universe having a beginning and an end. All our religions have creation myths, and even our natural sciences are based on this assumption.

Judaism, Christianity and Islam are prophetic religions that, during the course of history, are waiting—or have waited for—their Messiah. We look outside. The world that is perceived through the senses is of primary importance to us; we think analytically and divide units into ever smaller sub-units. This is why we are becoming "specialists," people who know more and more about less and less. Our highly advanced sciences were born out of this way of thinking. Then, Einstein's theory of relativity came along and the realization of physicists that time and space are an inseparable unit, that space is "curved" and our universe is indeed limitless, but not infinite, and our concept of the world started to falter.

In the East, the paths to realization were always based on the view that what we call "time" stands still, in the "now." We do understand that everything that has ever happened—and will ever happen—happens in the "here and now." Could anything ever happen even a fraction of a second before or after the "now"? The "now" is the directly experienced part of what we call the "course of time." The concept of "before" and "after" is already a reflection of our brain. Saint Augustinus expresses exactly that: "Time consists of a triple present: the present as we experience it, the past as a present memory and the future as a present expectation."

It is quite astonishing that even the Western philosopher Wittgenstein, at one point in his writings, comes to the following conclusion: "If one understands eternity not as an infinite time span but as 'non-time,' then he who lives in the present lives forever."

The Two Great Religious Currents
of Humanity

VEDIC RELIGIONS

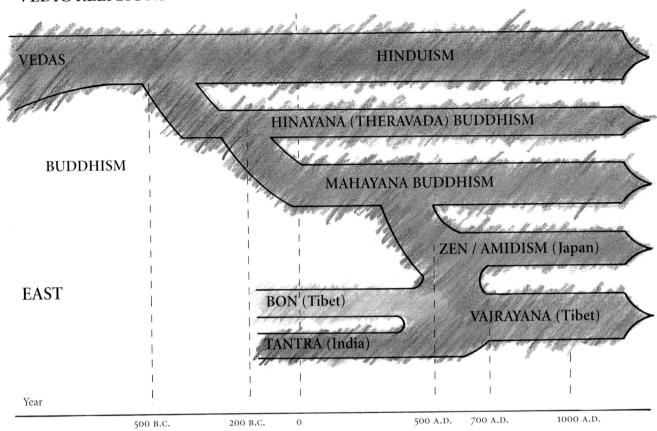

VEDAS

HINDUISM

HINAYANA (THERAVADA) BUDDHISM

BUDDHISM

MAHAYANA BUDDHISM

ZEN / AMIDISM (Japan)

EAST

BON (Tibet)

VAJRAYANA (Tibet)

TANTRA (India)

Year

| 500 B.C. | 200 B.C. | 0 | 500 A.D. | 700 A.D. | 1000 A.D. |

ABRAHAMIC RELIGIONS

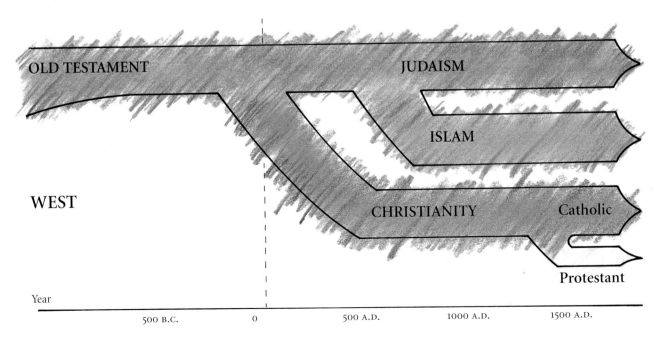

OLD TESTAMENT

JUDAISM

ISLAM

WEST

CHRISTIANITY

Catholic

Protestant

Year

| 500 B.C. | 0 | 500 A.D. | 1000 A.D. | 1500 A.D. |

In the beginning was the word

This well-known passage is found in the prologue to the Gospel of St. John: "In the beginning was the word and the word was God, and God was the word. Everything originated from it, and without it nothing has come about." I found a passage analogous to this in one of the oldest Indian scriptures, the *Rig-Veda*, whose origins are lost in 2000 B.C.: "In the beginning there was no being, but there was also no non-being, there was neither death nor life. Only the One was breathing without breathing, nothing was yet separate from him."

Both texts are trying to describe something that is actually indescribable—a paradox, something irrational, something illogical, something that is incomprehensible for the mind. It reads as: "In the beginning there was no being…," and our mind immediately deduces: "So it was non-being!" The text then continues: "There was also no non-being." Both states do not exist—neither the state of being nor the state of non-being. The mind is in a way short-circuited. The same situation is described by: "In the beginning was the word, and the word was God, and outside of the word, outside of God, there was nothing." Astrophysicists believe that our universe was created by a "big bang." There are already publications on this topic that are thicker than the *Holy Bible* and that describe everything that supposedly happened in the first second after the big bang. The opening of one of the popular scientific books is: "In the beginning there was hydrogen!" But up to now, no one has dared to ask the question, what happened before the big bang? Isn't this the most fascinating question of all? One second before the big bang there was NOTHINGNESS. Not a normal NOTHINGNESS though, because, as we all know, nothing can come out of NOTHINGNESS. It has to have been a NOTHINGNESS that was not yet different from itself and outside of which there was nothing else. A primordial potential, a first-class absurdity: a NOTHINGNESS, out of which the ALL can manifest itself. The only scientific and logical answer to this confusing and, for the sciences, upsetting question concerning the second before would probably be that this question is inadmissible and may not be asked. Logically there was no time before the big bang and therefore also "no second before." This does represent a small victory of the mind, but the mystery still remains.

Brahman, Atman and Trimurti

The holy scriptures of India, the *Vedas*, call this original state *Brahman*. Brahman is the original, the absolute, the eternal primordial force existing of itself. It is the cosmic force that is inherent in everything. And it is the totally unpersonal or rather suprapersonal, that which is not yet structured in any way, that which has no characteristics, is beyond time and space and cannot be comprehended by the intellect. Out of that which cannot be talked about nor described, out of the ALL-NOTHINGNESS, arises what the Indians call *Atman*: the indestructible self in man, the "inner light." "Atman" is a Sanskrit word. This ancient language belongs to the Indo-European language group and is related to German. You can hear the German words *Atem*, *Odem*, and *Lebensodem*, i.e. "the breath of life," in the word "Atman."

God blew the breath of life into Adam. Atman is therefore life, the central point of all that is. Its source is the all-consciousness Brahman.

According to the Indian concept, after life is breathed into man—after this act of creation—a trinity is created: the beginning, the end and, in between the two, the duration. We cannot conceive of anything in creation that does not have a beginning and an end. And we cannot imagine a beginning and an end without a third element in between, the duration. The Indians call this threefold state *Trimurti*: three in one and one in three, a kind of holy trinity. As soon as the divine potential enters creation, the trinity is born: Brahma, Vishnu and Shiva. These are the gods that personify becoming, being and dissolving. Brahma is the creator of the world (not to be confused with Brahman, the Absolute), Vishnu is the preserver of the world, and Shiva is the destroyer of the world.

This is the magnetic field of creation, the positive and the negative, and in between is the "arc of light," the world as we experience it through our senses—the veil, *Maya*, through which we perceive the world. The positive is spring, the beginning. The negative is autumn, the end. No beginning is conceivable without a prior end. Beginning and end are fundamentally neutral; the positive is not better than the negative; both are two extremes of reality. The Chinese call this "yes-no," by which they mean "the absolute." Only the pairs of opposites together make up the whole: light-dark, up-down, suffering-joy. When I say "white," I am also implying "black," and the concept of "non-duality" (Sanskrit, *advaita*) is, at the same time, faced by "non-unity," i.e. "duality."

The concept of non-duality

As was already mentioned, the *Vedas* are the Indian books of knowledge. The philosophy that derived from them is called Vedanta philosophy (*veda* = "knowledge," *anta* = "end," the "end of knowledge"). The ultimate conclusion Vedanta philosophy reaches is called *advaita*, absolute "non-duality." This is the end of knowledge: words and thoughts cease in the pre-creative original state in which the word was still with God, and God himself was the word. Non-duality is NOTHINGNESS that encompasses EVERYTHING. It is the Nirvana of Lord Buddha, provided that this state of "non-duality" becomes a living reality in the consciousness of man, as we shall soon see.

Reincarnation and karma

Before we can talk about the teachings of Buddha we need to have a look at the meaning of reincarnation and karma. Only then can we understand what he wants to liberate us from with his doctrine. Reincarnation is about rebirth. It is closely linked to the concept of karma, which could be translated as "destiny" in our language, a destiny that we create ourselves and that is based on cause and effect, thus keeping the cycle of rebirth in motion.

Within the magnetic field of creation, all beings, humans, animals and even plants are constantly coming and going in an eternal rhythm. In an infinite evolutionary process, mind develops from unconsciousness to consciousness. A process of awakening takes place during countless lifetimes as a plant, an animal and finally as a human being. "God is sleeping in the stone, breathing in the plant, dreaming in the animal and waking up in man" is a sentence by Angelus Silesius that sounds like an Indian proverb.

In the scriptures this cycle of rebirth is called *samsara*. The death of a person is thus not considered to be something final. Death is a kind of sleep through which we lose our body. The question of where and how we go between death and the next reincarnation simultaneously raises the question where and how we go after sinking into deep sleep. Where are we when we sleep without dreaming?

The later Vedic tradition talks about rebirth, about the possibility to continue whatever we started in countless successive lifetimes. The law of evolution is applied to the individual in a logical way, concluding that he or she does not disappear after death but has the opportunity to carry on, in a new "shell," from the same point where his development was interrupted by the loss of the old body; albeit without any memory of previous lives, although equipped with the sum of all the experiences gained in previous lives. And his unfulfilled desires, his cravings and his thirst for life always make him look for a new maternal womb, a new incarnation on earth.

On his path through countless lifetimes, man is accompanied by his karma. This is not a destiny that was intended by a "higher force," or thrust upon us from the outside, but a destiny created entirely by us. Karma is the law of cause and effect and is understood very rationally as a law; thus, it is free of judgment. You could, of course, put things very simply and say: "A good deed reaps good karma; a bad deed reaps bad karma." But the consequences of our deeds are to be considered neither a punishment nor a reward coming from a higher, judging force. "As you make your bed, so you must lie" is a Western proverb that refers to our deeds and attitudes in our present life. We tend to make higher forces, or the forces of destiny, responsible for strokes of fate or even strokes of luck, if we cannot understand their causes in our life.

Death does not interrupt the law of cause and effect, just as our nightly sleep cannot protect us tomorrow from the repercussions of today's deeds. And just as the law of our actions binds us to cause and effect, so everything happening in the world must be understood as the result of a causality akin to physical laws. We have to remember, however, that the forces that cause karma are not only found in the past, but also in the future. Our intended deeds affect our karma as if they had already taken place. The freedom of human will is founded on this realization.

The great Indian epics

We are still in the world of pre-Buddhist Hinduism. It is here necessary to describe this philosophy in detail so as to get to know the soil on which Buddhism was able to flourish. When talking about Hinduism, we must not fail to mention the two powerful epics: the *Mahabharata* and the *Ramayana*. In these epics the depth of Vedantic philosophy is illustrated for ordinary people in an almost never-ending sequence of tales. At this point, I would like to tell one of my favorite stories, so that readers can feel the superbly edifying power inherent in these stories. I put the second and the most beautiful one at the end of these expositions. These stories are, of course, only brief vignettes from an extensive epic.

The Goddess Ganga and the King's Son

Ganga, the female spirit of the holy river Ganges, was called upon to help bring a karma to fruition, and for this purpose she took on the body of a woman of celestial beauty. She walked up and down the bank of her river and was soon discovered by a young prince who was hunting in the woods nearby. Her bewitching fragrance had shown him the way.

Enamored of her at first sight, he asked the beauty to accompany him to his palace. Ganga did not refuse, but she did make some conditions. One of them was that he had to decide whether he wanted to possess her "from her belt upwards" or "from her belt down." Both at the same time was not possible.

The young man went home and was very confused. He tossed and turned in his bed all night and couldn't fall asleep. He found himself in a terrible dilemma; he knew what he wanted, but he also knew what he should do, and so he kept on fighting with himself until dawn.

Once the sun rose, he went to the banks of the river and said, "Mother, I have made a decision. I would like to possess you from your belt upwards." At that Ganga smiled, loosened her belt and let it fall to the ground; thus everything was included "from the belt upwards!" "From the belt upwards" means the spiritual; "from the belt downwards" means the material.

Whoever chooses the spiritual has chosen everything, the spiritual as well as the material resulting from it. If the prince had decided differently, what would have been left for him after the belt had fallen to the ground? A philosophical truth communicated through that kind of imagery is able to penetrate very deeply into the human soul and from there to unfold its authentic message.

Prince Siddharta Gautama

Gautama Buddha was born into this religious climate. He came into the world in the middle of the 6th century B.C. as the son of a minor prince in Northern India. He was known as Prince Siddharta, Siddharta Gautama of the House of Sakya. A white elephant announced the birth of a son to his mother Maya in a dream, and she had a virginal birth; the child was born out of the side of her body. She died only a few days later. The prince was raised by his mother's sister. His father tried to shield his son from all earthly suffering by making his life in the palace as pleasant as possible. Indeed, he was thoroughly pampered and coddled.

At age sixteen he was married but continued taking part in games and competitions with his peers. After thirteen years of marriage his wife presented him with a child, a boy named Rahula. The only restriction on his life of worldly pleasures was his father's order that he was not to go beyond the walls of the palace gardens. But the young man grew weary of the luxury and sensual pleasures. The desire to get to know the world at large grew ever stronger in him. So, one day, Siddharta asked his friend and confidant, the chariot driver Chandaka, to secretly take him into town without letting his father know. The famous fable *The Four Outings* tells us the story.

The "Four Outings"

During the first outing, Siddharta meets an old man; he learns that all humans grow old. During the second outing, he meets a sick man, and during the third, he witnesses the cremation of a corpse. When, during the fourth outing, he meets a begging monk and learns from his servant Chandaka that the monk left his home and became a homeless person in order to find an answer beyond illness, old age and death, the prince's decision is made: he, too, will leave the illusory happiness of worldly pleasures and seek the truth.

The Great Departure

The "great departure," this important event in the life of the Buddha, is told in the *Pali* canon as follows: The prince said to his devoted servant Chandaka, "Wake up my horse and get it ready so quietly that nobody hears you."

Chandaka replied, "The night is not a good time for traveling; it is not the right time for a ride. No enemy seems to want to attack the palace. I don't understand why I should saddle the horse so carefully tonight."

The prince said, "Don't you know that great enemies are threatening us? These enemies are old age, sickness and death. These are great enemies. Saddle the horse quickly so that nobody can stop us or hold us back." The servant prepared the horse at once and led it into the courtyard of the palace. He then said, "The horse is ready!"

The prince wanted to mount it, but the horse whinnied sadly. The gods were worried that difficulties would arise. So they stifled the neighing of the horse lest somebody would hear it. The prince mounted the horse and rode out the back door of the palace, which miraculously had opened on its own. The canon then tells how the future Buddha, in a forest outside of town, exchanged his princely garb for the tattered clothes of a hunter who happened to cross his path. He then said goodbye to his companion and to his favorite horse and went off into the world to lead the life of a poor mendicant.

The seven-year apprenticeship

Siddharta Gautama was on the road for seven years in order to learn from different masters everything the yogis, scholars and sages knew in those days. He studied all the holy scriptures and eventually even practiced the strictest form of asceticism, refusing any kind of food for a long time.

Once he had lost so much weight that he looked like a skeleton, he realized that this path was not the right one either. In his teachings he is quoted as having said, "These severe deprivations will not help me go beyond the human laws; I will not attain true realization through them." However, in a country like India where extreme self-castigations were highly regarded, he had to undergo such trials as well. Eventually the nascent Buddha discovered the path of contemplation, the path without a path: meditation. And this path led him to his goal.

Enlightenment

During the seventh year of his quest and wanderings, Siddharta Gautama finally settled down in the shadow of a pipal tree and made a vow not to leave until he had attained true realization. And thus he sat in deep meditation under the fig tree for seven days. Then, during a full-moon night, possibly in the year 533 B.C., Siddharta Gautama, the prince of the royal house of the Sakyas, became Gautama Buddha—Gautama, "the fully awakened one," the ENLIGHTENED ONE.

Mara's temptations

A popular legend tells us that the great ruler of the underworld, Mara, the "Lord of lust and earthly pleasures," saw his empire threatened. He mobilized his most terrifying demons and sent them after the Enlightened One. But the swords, arrows, spears and axes they flung at him floated to the ground like a shower of flower petals.

Mara finally resorted to his most powerful weapon. He had his three daughters with the names Desire, Tenderness and Sensuality perform a veiled dance in front of the Enlightened One. In vain! The inner peace of the Buddha triumphed over his seductresses, who threw themselves at his feet in reverence when they saw that he remained steadfast.

93 • *Victory.*

The Four Noble Truths

The realizations which the Buddha attained during his enlightenment and which were to become the foundation of his teachings are of far-reaching importance yet amazingly simple. He announced them during his first famous sermon in Sarnath near Benares (the Indian city called Varanasi today).

His first listeners were his former companions who had earlier left him out of disappointment when he had abandoned his asceticism. And they still resented him, believing that he had gone back to his old, worldly ways. They made a pact to show him no respect by remaining seated when he arrived. Yet when the Enlightened One stepped before them, they were overcome by deep religious feelings and threw themselves at his feet. It was here, in the Deer Park at Sarnath that Gautama the Buddha transmitted the teachings on the Four Noble Truths.

The First Noble Truth is: "Everything is suffering: birth is suffering; illness is suffering; death is suffering; being in the company of unloved ones is suffering; separation from loved ones is suffering; non-fulfillment of desires is suffering." Everything is transitory; everything that was created must come to an end. But are there not also beautiful and good things in this world? What about happiness? Is it also suffering? In a way—the realization that suffering permeates our entire existence is inexorable; everything that was ever created has to come to an end sometime, and the more beautiful, the happier it was, the more painful the end. That is the first truth of the Four Noble Truths.

The Second Noble Truth investigates the cause of suffering. Why is it that everything is permeated by suffering? What is the reason—how can this be? The Enlightened One says: "This, you monks, is the holy truth regarding the origin of suffering: it is the craving for life that leads us from one rebirth to another, it is the craving for lust, the thirst for becoming something, the thirst for power." And this craving, this desire, is born out of ignorance, and out of ignorance is born hatred, the opposite of love, which in turn leads to suffering. This is the Second Noble Truth.

Now that the cause of suffering has been determined, we have to resolve to completely destroy the roots of this cause. "This, you monks, is the holy truth regarding the liberation from suffering—the removal of this craving through the total elimination of desire. You have to let go of it, get rid of it, free yourself of it and not allow it another opportunity." This is the Third Noble Truth.

But how should we do this? How can we let go of this craving for life? How can we let go of it, get rid of it, free ourself of it and not allow it another opportunity? The Venerable One says: "This, monks, is the holy truth regarding the path leading to the elimination of suffering. It is the holy eightfold path: correct view, correct resolve, correct speech, correct action, correct way of life, correct aspiration, correct awareness and correct self-immersion." This Eightfold Path, the fourth of the Noble Truths, is quite logical and consistent. a quality which we encounter in Buddhism again and again.

94 • The "Wheel of Dharma," with its eight spokes, is the fundamental symbol of all of the Buddhist traditions.

The Eightfold Path

The first point is the correct view. One needs to recognize, to understand something, to have an insight. This is something we try to do all the time in our daily life. We sometimes say, "Yes, that's probably the way it is." We recognize the connections we did not see up to now. Something dawns on us, and this insight makes us happy.

This then leads to correct resolve. The correct insight on its own is not sufficient. We must take the appropriate steps based on this insight, or else the insight is of no use. That is the second point of the Eightfold Path. The third point is correct speech. If we have made the correct decision on the basis of the correct view, we will speak differently.

Correct action then naturally arises out of correct speech, and that leads to the fifth point, correct way of life. A new way of life will surely follow when we begin to think differently, speak differently and act differently. The sixth point is correct aspiration or endeavor. It is about attaining new insights through a conscious effort, which correct awareness, the seventh step of the Eightfold Path, should bring about.

Now we are coming to the core of the entire Buddhist doctrine, the eighth and last step of the path: correct self-immersion. While practicing this contemplation, this meditation which is the main practice of the Buddha's teaching, we gather new strength, attain new insights and understanding, and are enlightened by new realizations which lead us back to correct decision and correct speech. The eightfold path is thus a self-contained cycle.

Gautama Buddha shows us this path of salvation, the path leading to liberation from suffering. And yet, Buddha is not a "savior" in the Christian sense of the word, but rather a "guide." His teachings are a tool, a "vehicle" or "raft" as it is called in the scriptures—"good for taking you across, but not for carrying you."

As is to be expected, the words and deeds of the Enlightened One have an impact on the behavior and the ethics of Buddhists. For example, the scriptures mention an incident in which meat was placed in the Buddha's begging bowl during his rounds. A Buddhist should "not harm any sentient being" and consequently should not kill. So, strictly speaking, he should not eat meat. The Buddha, however, ate the meat which a blacksmith had offered him. When his disciples pointed out this contradiction to him and asked how they should interpret his behavior, he answered, "The blacksmith gave his best, and if someone gives his best, it should not be rejected." He thus valued respect for the good intention of the donor higher than the commandment not to eat meat.

The actual teachings are, however, intertwined and sometimes even obscured by countless legends, which found a rich soil in the Indian climate of that time and which sometimes convey wonderful truths.

The legend of the robber Angulimala

During his wanderings the Buddha once came to the edge of a deep forest. The people warned him and said he should not go through this forest, because the robber Angulimala, who was feared by everybody for miles around, lived there. It was said that Angulimala robbed and killed any travelers, and that it was most unwise to enter this forest. But the Buddha did not let this well-meant advice prevent him from proceeding into the forest.

It did not take long for Angulimala to spot him. He shouted in a terrible voice, "Stay where you are, wanderer, or I will throw my spear!" The Buddha serenely walked on, not paying any attention to the threat. "Stop or I will kill you!" Angulimala screamed in rage. When the Buddha did not heed this demand either, the robber threw one spear, and then a second and a third, but they all missed their target! Utterly confused and angry at having missed, Angulimala screamed at the wanderer one last time, "You miserable wretch, don't you know who I am? I am Angulimala, the greatest of robbers, the terror of the forest; my voice alone instills the fear of death in humans. So stand still!" Thereupon the Buddha turned around, gave Angulimala a stern but compassionate look and said, "I am standing, Angulimala, I am standing. But you are running!" Angulimala just stood there, thunderstruck. Was it not true what the fearless stranger had said? Was the stranger not standing on firm ground, calm and free, while he, Angulimala, was chasing after an illusionary happiness that he would never be able to attain through robbing and killing?

The legend goes on to tell how the terrible robber Angulimala burst into tears, threw himself at the Buddha's feet and begged him to take him on as his disciple. Even as a disciple Angulimala almost certainly remained a wild and untamable fellow, but now he was fighting for the good. In a flash he had had the correct view and made the correct decision. He also found the correct speech, which was undoubtedly followed by the correct action and finally by the correct way of life.

Buddhism, an atheist religion?

Up to now, we have only talked about an Enlightened One and a path of salvation, but not about a God—not about an absolute God nor a God-Father. Also not about a God as the creator of every earthly thing. We became acquainted with Atman through Hinduism, and Atman probably is the closest notion to a "God-Father." We also heard about Brahman, that which is unpersonal, unpronounceable and causal and which could best be compared with the Christian notion of the "divine original source." Buddhism only talks about the realization of suffering and the path of liberation. There is no God as a creator, nor a God-Father as a prerequisite for the teachings. Buddha focuses his attention totally on man. He teaches self-liberation. According to the original Buddhist teachings, no help can come from the outside, nor is any grace to be expected.

Insight takes the place of belief. The notion of "sin" cannot exist either. There is no outside authority that judges or condemns our actions. There are only meritorious or reprehensible deeds, according to the concept of cause and effect rather than according to moral values. These actions create our karma that binds us to the eternal cycle of rebirth for an unforeseeable period of time. We have the opportunity to recognize this cycle and to liberate ourselves from it by practicing loving kindness and by accepting everything that exists without discrimination.

Nirvana, the great "Nothingness"

The only thing that is considered as absolute in Buddhism is Nothingness, EMPTINESS. We have come across this paradoxical concept before—in the Holy Scriptures in the passages that try to describe the state before creation, in astrophysics with the question about the "second before the big bang" and in the unsuccessful attempt to explain in words the absolute Brahman.

The teachings say: "What is the vehicle? Is the axle the vehicle, or the shaft—or the wheels? In reality, the vehicle does not exist." We could go on and ask, "What is the wheel? Is the wheel the tires, the spokes, the hub?" In reality, the wheel does not exist either. Everything that was ever created really does not exist, at least not as we perceive it with our senses. The senses function like a filter or a veil (the veil of the Goddess Maya); we no longer see phenomena as they are but as they are conveyed to us by our senses.

Thus, according to the Buddhist view, there are two levels of truth: the truth that describes the phenomena as they appear and the truth that discovers their true essence. The first truth describes how the river flows to the ocean and concludes that the river exists. However, a Buddhist may also ask the confusing question, "Is it possible to bathe in the same river twice?" And the river disappears, because it is neither the water nor the river bank. The only thing that we can say about the river, without even thinking along Buddhist lines, is the fact that it is a continuum. And that is exactly what Buddhism says about creation—it is a continuum that is ever-changing, constantly dissolving and never existing in the way in which we define it.

A seeker who is following the Buddhist path will one day experience the great disappointment. The last illusion, the sensory illusion, is taken away, and that which remains is NOTHINGNESS, NON-BEING—Nirvana. *Nir* is a "negation" and *vana* is derived from "blowing, to blow away." Where is the flame when the candle has gone out? Blown out. Where is the summer during the winter? Where does the darkness go when the light comes on? They all disappear, blow away, and yet they are present without being perceived. The following parable will "bring light" into this NOTHINGNESS that embraces everything.

The parable of the extinct flame

A novice carrying a butter lamp walks through the monastery and is being asked by a visitor, "Son, tell me where this flame comes from?" The young monk contemplates the flame, blows it out and says, "If you tell me where it just went, I will tell you where it comes from."

This brilliant and at the same time profound answer may delight us. But where did the flame that was there just a minute ago really go? The flame is now in a state that is beyond polarity and that could be called the void. It does not have any qualities anymore. It would make no sense to say that it is everywhere and nowhere, timeless, spaceless or immortal. And yet, the flame exists. How else could we light it again, bring it back into creation, into the "here and now"?

From the Buddhist point of view, nirvana and samsara (that which is blown away and that which is created) are both but two aspects of the One Reality.

The Tibetan practice of visualization

Tibetan monks know a meditation practice that can illustrate what may be understood as this so-called "emptiness." The first stage of the practice consists of memorizing a religious image very carefully and in great detail, to sort of "learn the image by heart." In the second stage the memorized image is visualized, i.e. we imagine the picture in front of our "inner eye" and try to hold it as long and intensively as possible. In doing so, we should not be distracted even for a fraction of a second. We must focus on the image with our entire being and slowly become identical with it. Subject and object will disappear. In the third phase, the visualized image is slowly and carefully dissolved from the outside, starting with the contours. We slowly make it disappear until nothing is left—nothing except for our presence, our being in the present, in the here and now.

Needless to say, this is extremely difficult for us. Because of our Western education we are not at all used to simply "being" without being "somebody" at the same time. But it is precisely this NOTHINGNESS—that can only be experienced through "being"—that we are dealing with if we want to understand the essence of the Buddhist teachings. The nothingness, the emptiness, is the gateway to the unimaginable timeless and spaceless state of nirvana.

The fulfillment of the teachings

The teachings are being fulfilled in this state of timeless and spaceless being. Suffering needs time and space in order to unfold. No suffering is possible in the infinite here and eternal now; but there is also no bliss and no divine happiness! If bliss and happiness were the characteristics of nirvana, they would have to end just like everything else that is, and would eventually turn into suffering.

The change from the "Small Vehicle" (Hinayana) to the "Greater Vehicle" (Mahayana)

The original doctrine focused very much on the monk orders. It was an ascetic path and, as we have seen, elitist and not for the common people. Of course, no doctrine can be too popular if it demands that the practice start with and by oneself. We are always full of good ideas for our fellow human beings, and we know exactly who would have to do what better so that we could achieve an earthly paradise. But starting with ourself? Why with ourself? There is hardly anything to improve…

Because of this perceived difficulty, the Buddha's teachings became almost totally extinct until the beginning of our era. At that time, the original "Small Vehicle" (*Hinayana*) changed into the "Greater Vehicle" (*Mahayana*). The concept of brotherly love, infinite compassion (*karuna*) and loving kindness (*metta*) was created. The idea gained acceptance that there must be beings out there who, shortly before their fulfillment, do not take the final step into nirvana, beings who voluntarily refuse to find liberation in nirvana and instead, as "Buddha candidates" and out of compassion for all unliberated beings, decide to work for their well-being.

95 • *The Bodhisattva Manjusri, the "Guardian of Wisdom."*

Due to this change in Buddhist thinking the ideal of the Bodhisattva was born. The "Small Vehicle" developed into the "Greater Vehicle."

When we think of how much of the time available to us is used to solve our own problems and how little time is left for helping others, we are able to realize how far removed we still are from the state of a Bodhisattva. Many people cannot even cope with their own problems and are dependent on others for help. A Bodhisattva, however, is an ideal being who does not have any personal problems. Free of all personal attachments and filled with deep compassion for all of those beings who have not yet found the path, he is totally selfless and makes himself available as a "friend in need." Gautama Buddha was a living example of this path of human evolution. He collected all earthly experiences as Prince Siddharta; then freed himself of all personal human problems as a seeking ascetic; and finally, as an enlightened being, he postponed his own entry into nirvana in order to serve suffering humanity.

Thus, in the course of many centuries, a transcendental heaven with countless Bodhisattvas has opened up. These Bodhisattvas are worshiped with the same reverence as our Christian saints. It is at this point that Buddhism changes from a doctrine for monks and ascetics to a real religion, a religion that is also intended for ordinary people. The newly evolved Bodhisattvas can be depicted just like the gods of old. Offerings can be made to them; they can be loved, worshipped, invoked. You can pray to them and visualize them. In this way Bodhisattvas become bridges, mediators or friends in need.

It was in this form that Buddhism arrived in Tibet in the 7th century A.D. The meeting of Mahayana and the locally prevailing Bon religion produced a very interesting type of Buddhism. On its way to the East, the "Great Doctrine" had already made its way through China to Japan. And in Zen Buddhism it finally rid itself of the ballast accumulated on the long journey and thus purified itself. Even the logical way of thinking that is so characteristic, especially in the original teachings, is shed. In Zen only the inconceivable paradox has validity.

It should be added that the "Small Vehicle" (Hinayana), or Theravada Buddhism as the original doctrine is called, has remained alive up to the present in Sri Lanka (formerly Ceylon) and in most Indo-Chinese countries. It still does not include any rituals, and the begging monks have no specific function other than to be examples for ordinary religious people. The Perfect One does not become a Bodhisattva who compassionately helps others but an *Arhat*, one who is on the path to liberate himself.

Vajrayana, the "Diamond Vehicle"

Let us now follow Buddhism in its form as the "Great Vehicle" on its northbound journey, which, during the middle of the 1st century A.D., spread across the entire Himalayan region all the way into the heart of Mongolia and once again transformed itself to become the tantric form of Buddhism, Vajrayana.

A quote from Gautama Buddha can basically be applied to all the later Buddhist schools: "Do not rely on hearsay, nor on traditions, nor on the opinions of the day, nor on the authority of the holy scriptures, nor simply on rational grounds and logical conclusions, nor on made-up theories and favored opinions, nor on the impression of personal preferences, nor on the authority of a master! Only when you yourself have realized that these things are healing and impeccable, create understanding, and, when executed, result in blessings and well-being, then you may adopt them. What I just said was said precisely in that regard."

What statement could make us more aware of the fact that Buddhism is not a credo but a doctrine of realization? When a student calculates the lengths of the sides of a triangle with the help of the theorem of Pythagoras, he does not do it because he has professed belief in this theory. Rather, he sees the connections, recognizes the logic hidden in the theorem and applies it. By recognizing that the theorem is correct, the truth formulated by Pythagoras becomes his own personal truth. He could continue to apply it without any difficulties, even if it were proven that the theorem was not indeed fom Pythagoras, which, incidentally, seems to be all but certain today.

At a scientific conference on the phenomena of "Time and Space" that was attended by leading physicists, the Dalai Lama said, "My religion is not only about love and loving kindness, it is also the religion of the atomic age." This truly bold statement by a man who is regarded as the guardian of one of the oldest religious traditions came as totally unexpected for Western listeners and made headlines in the press. Since a Buddhist does not support a dogma or a credo, he can indeed make this statement; he is following the "path of realization" just as consequently as science does. This fundamental attitude committed to "Nothingness" has made it possible for the Buddhist doctrine of realization to repeatedly take on new forms in the course of history.

The "Diamond Vehicle," *Vajrayana*, the third and latest form of Buddhism, differentiates itself from the "Greater Vehicle," Mahayana, above all because it includes the sexual energies of man on the path, similar to the Indian practice of Shaktism. The Shaktas worship the force of creation that sustains the universe and that manifests itself on an earthly plane as sexual energy. The symbolism of Shaktism and Tantrism is therefore of a sexual nature, and the deities are often depicted in sexual union (in Tibetan, *yab-yum*).

The tantric scriptures—which are basically considered secret—consist of two schools: the path of *Vamacara* (the left-hand path), that physically enacts the sexual union of the deities in form of a strictly secret ritual, and the *Dakshinacara* (the right-hand path), that enacts the union purely on a spiritual level and in which the sexual forms of expression are merely symbols for the meditative process. "Left-hand tantrism" is always regarded as dangerous. Without extremely strict spiritual discipline, it certainly does not lead to the desired experience of the ultimate reality, i.e. enlightenment, but instead to unbridled rites and sexual excesses.

Both schools are part of Tibetan Buddhism. We who are educated in a Western way first have to free ourselves of the concept that sexuality and everything associated with it is sinful. Since Buddhism does not recognize a God and therefore no judging higher authority, the Christian concept of sin in the broadest sense is missing. Yet there are "beneficial" and "harmful" actions. The beneficial ones lead us to the divine, the oneness; the harmful ones take us away from what is whole, what is sacred. If we see it this way, we must ask ourselves the question why the profound experience of sexual union between a man and a woman seems "harmful" to us. From a Buddhist point of view only the reciprocal inflicting of suffering is truly "harmful." Wouldn't this insight be a step on the "path of realization"?

In the Tibetan form of Buddhism, other elements have been integrated into the tantric path—elements of the Bon religion which, in pre-Buddhist times, was the prevailing religion on the "roof of the world." It is almost impossible to trace back the origins of the animistic/shamanistic forms of religion practiced by these mountain people; they have taken on too much of Buddhism in the past 1700 years. In a way, they have become a mirror image. We can only guess at the origins of the old magical Bon belief. Buddhism did integrate the outer form of some of the Bon rituals but changed their inner meaning. What is so fascinating about the later development of Tibetan Buddhism is its almost inexhaustible abundance of forms of expression. Its imagery is just as diverse as "the sand in the Ganges." Its iconography alone can hardly be grasped in its entirety. What is left is the original Buddhist insight that everything is only a different facet of the "One Reality," *sunyata*. And that is beyond the realm of concepts.

The four schools of Tibetan Buddhism

In an earlier chapter, we already learned how Buddhism came to the "roof of the world" in the first half of the 7th century A.D. Still today, there exist essentially four schools or teaching traditions which, in part, differ considerably from each other with regard to their rituals and the interpretation of the scriptures.

The oldest tradition is the Nyingma tradition, literally meaning "School of the Elders." It transmits the Buddhist teachings that Padmasambhava brought to Tibet from India in the 8th century. The Nyingmapas consider *Dzog-chen*, the "Great Perfection," to be the most important teaching, and its followers see it as the purest and most secret of Buddha Sakyamuni's teachings. The basic assumption of *Dzog-chen* is that the "naked" or "normal" mind is immaculate and pure in essence. This direct insight interrupts cyclic existence. The early Nyingmapas were laymen as well as monks. Named after their ceremonial hats, they belong to the "Red Hats."

The second school, which is also associated with the "Red Hats," is the Kagyu school (its followers are Kagyupas). In this school some of the highest teachings of the *Vajrayana* are transmitted, the *Mahamudra* ("Great Seal") teachings that are related to Zen Buddhism. The *Mahamudra* teachings of the Indian master Tilopa were transmitted as a meditation system via Naropa and Marpa, the "translator," to Milarepa. The practice starts out with the *samatha* meditation described on page 146, which is the "meditative path leading to spiritual tranquility," and ends with the experience of emptiness and absolute clarity. Today the Kagyu school, especially the Karma Kagyu branch (the "oral lineage of the Karmapas"), is among the most successful Buddhist orders in the West.

The Sakya order, also part of the tradition of the "Red Hats," is named after the Sakya monastery in western Tibet. Five great scholars who were all considered incarnations of the Bodhisattva Manjusri founded the teaching tradition during the 12th and 13th centuries. We already mentioned its most famous representatives, Sakya Pandita and his nephew Pagpa, in an earlier chapter. The "throne-holders" (Sakya-Trinzin) who have traditionally come from the Khon dynasty, dedicate themselves above all to the teachings known as *Lamdre*, the "path to the goal."

The Indian scholar Atisha, who spent the last years of his life (1045–1055) in Tibet, founded the Kadampa school. After the reform brought about by Tsongkhapa, this school became the last of the four main schools, i.e. the great Gelugpa tradition, the "school of the virtuous ones." In order to set themselves apart from the unreformed traditions, the Gelugpas, who live according to strict monastic rules, wear yellow instead of red ceremonial hats, thus acquiring the popular name "Yellow Hats." The foundation of their teachings is essentially based on Tsongkhapa's commentaries to the *Madhyamika*, the "Middle Path." This "doctrine on emptiness" (*sunyata*) dates back to Nagarjuna (2nd/3rd century). Some famous representatives of this doctrine were Candrakirti, Santiraksita and Kamalasila. During the 17th century the Gelugpa school also took over the political leadership of the country under the "Great 5th" Dalai Lama.

In spite of these different schools of thought, a real split between them never occurred. All the different orders agree that, when it comes to the final realization, the goal is the realization of the ultimate truth and that the path is compassion and loving kindness for all "sentient beings."

Yudhistira and the dog

I would like to conclude these somewhat dry theoretical explanations, as promised, with a legend from pre-Buddhist times. It is from the *Mahabharata* epic and is valid for all times:

> The great hero Yudhistira had come to the conclusion that there was nothing left to keep him in this world. He had experienced all the joys, all the power and all the honors that a man can have. But he had also gone through all the earthly hells, had experienced poverty, bondage, banishment and humiliation.
>
> Since he had arrived at the end of his mission in life, he set out on his last journey and wandered towards the Himalayas, hoping to find the way to heaven from the highest mountain of the world. His family accompanied him part of the way, but soon one after another fell behind. One of them died of thirst in the extreme heat of the plains, another died of a fever in the tropical jungle. Yet others succumbed to fatigue or the cold once they started climbing into the icy heights. Thus, the group became smaller and smaller until Yudhistira was finally alone except for a small, faithful dog which had run after him from one of the last villages. When they reached the top of the mountain, the gateway to heaven opened up and Indra, the King of the Gods, came out and welcomed Yudhistira. But when he wanted to get into the fiery celestial vehicle that was to take him to heaven, the little dog also jumped in. Indra, the King of the Gods, indignantly refused to take along the dog and told Yudhistira to chase away this lice-ridden animal. Startled, Yudhistira paused and said, "Oh great Lord, this dog is the only soul that was faithful to me and followed me all the way. How can I leave him behind?"
>
> Then a big dispute arose between Yudhistira and the Lord of Heaven. But Indra could not be moved, and Yudhistira only had the chance to go to heaven

without the dog or to forsake heaven altogether. So Yudhistira turned around and said, "Oh Lord, I will gladly forsake a heaven that is not big enough to make room for a dog's soul."

At that moment, the small dog transformed itself into a blinding light, and Yama, the God of Death and Compassion, stood before him. While his senses were failing, he heard a voice saying, "Yudhistira, oh Yudhistira, Compassionate One, that was your last trial!" And the gateways of the true heaven opened to exuberant jubilation, and everything was glory and splendor.

Are there "bridges" between the different religions?

If we were to look for really solid bridges between the religions, we would not find them on the outside. Well-meaning people attempt to do this time and time again, but this inevitably leads to cheap concessions, to compromises and to a watering-down of all of the teachings. Real bridges can only be found when we turn inwards. Every religion carries within it a kind of "eternal truth" to which no particular religious community may lay claim exclusively. This "eternal spark" belongs to everybody and is in a way the core teaching common to all religions.

Take the image of a wheel with spokes. The spokes are the religions—towards the outer rim of the wheel they get further away from each other; towards the hub they get closer. And directly in the center of each wheel there is an almost mystical point that stands still. That sounds totally paradoxical. But when we think about it, we realize that this point is necessary. Within this point all the otherwise diverging parts are one. The ancient Greeks would have called this "synthesis." This is the point of uncompromising communication. Here all the spokes of the wheel are one without canceling or blurring their function towards the outside. From here bridges lead from one religion to another via a transcendental point that is common to all of them. In this dimension that can only be conceived by the intuitive mind, in this "in-depth communication" as it was once called, all contradictions are dissolved without blurring the boundaries of the great doctrines and world religions.

This communication is silence, a silence without words or concepts.

Isn't the common language between the great religions love, all-encompassing, universal love? The love born out of the silence, the love that flows out of the center of our being—isn't that the language of the heart that is understood by all people at all times?

96 • Om mani padme hum. *"Om 'Jewel in the lotus'" is an attempted free translation of this prayer.*

The "jewel" symbolizes the active male principle in creation and at the same time signifies the "path" that can be described as "loving kindness." The "lotus" symbolizes the passive female cosmic principle and signifies "the highest wisdom." Together they represent the fulfillment of the teachings.

The tradition of tulkus

In Tibetan Buddhism, a person who has been recognized as the reincarnation of a deceased, highly realized teacher or lama is called a *tulku*. The tradition developed out of the *Trikaya* doctrine (see page 162), which believes that Buddhas and Bodhisattvas repeatedly reincarnate in a human body in order to help other human beings attain liberation. Thus, the Dalai Lamas are considered to be reincarnations of the transcendental Bodhisattva Chenresig (Sanskrit: *Avalokitesvara*), and the Panchen Rinpoches are actually seen as the emanation of the transcendental Buddha Amitabha. At the same time, they are the personal successors of their own earlier human existence.

It is a very ancient concept of the Hindu culture that a human being can simultaneously be the incarnation of a deity. This concept was institutionalized in Tibet for the first time in the early 13th century by the second Karmapa. After the death of the head of the Karma Kagyu school, the reincarnation of his stream of consciousness (*namshe*) was searched for in a small child, based on precise instructions the Karmapa had given before his death. When a particular child had passed all the tests and had also recognized people from his past life, he was recognized as the first Karmapa in a new human body. The tradition of the tulkus assumes that a highly evolved being does not only have the capacity to determine the time of his own death but also the power to influence the place, time and circumstances of his own next reincarnation.

Several tulku lineages have developed in the course of time, and today quite a few of them live in exile in India or the West. To the great surprise of the Tibetans themselves, some of their great masters have in recent times preferred to be reborn as European or American children. Such was the case of Lama Thupten Yeshe, who had already looked after Western students, mainly in the Kopan monastery in Nepal, and founded several Dharma centers, mostly in Europe. Three years after his death, he was found as the child of Spanish parents. His spiritual successor, Osel Rinpoche, is being educated by a private teacher in Switzerland, in the Tibetan center of Rabten Choling in Mont Pélérin, until he returns to his previous monastery in Nepal. Another case is that of Trinley Rinpoche, a former student of the great master Kalu Rinpoche, who was reborn as the child of French-American parents and discovered in France.

The first tulku recognized by the Dalai Lama and born in Switzerland, Shiwalha Rinpoche, was brought by his Tibetan parents to his ancestral monastery in India for his education as soon as he started school. Thousands of devotees will be paying homage to him in the future, because the young Shiwalha belongs to a very famous lineage—he is the spiritual emanation of the teacher Santideva. Santideva was teaching at Nalanda University in India during the 7th and 8th century and wrote a very important text, the *Bodhicaryavatara* ("Entry into the life leading to enlightenment") that is still being used today.

97 • *Ceremony during the official installation of the reincarnation of the Ven. Trijang Rinpoche in Ganden, his monastery, now rebuilt in India. This photograph was taken in the spring of 1988 in the Labrang temple. The stupa with the relics of the last Trijang Rinpoche is in the center. To the right is a picture of him in his last incarnation. The teacher of the boy, Lati Rinpoche, is sitting below the photograph.*

98 • Yongzin Trijang Rinpoche, the reincarnation of the Dalai Lama's former senior tutor, in a photo taken in 1988.

99 • Shiwalha
Rinpoche, the first
tulku to be found in
exile in Switzerland, in
a photo taken in 1985.
As a spiritual
emanation of the
famous teacher
Santideva, he belongs
to the tradition of the
Gelugpas and will
receive his spiritual
training at his previous
monastery in India.

100 • *Trinley Rinpoche in a photo taken in 1983. He is one of four white tulkus. In his former life as a Tibetan boy, he was a disciple of the Ven. Kalu Rinpoche and died at the early age of 16. In a letter that was opened after his death, he expressed his deepest desire to "come back" soon in order to be close to his beloved master. Since Kalu Rinpoche had been teaching in France, his reincarnation was searched for and discovered in his immediate surroundings and found as the child of white parents. Trinley belongs to the Kagyupa lineage.*

The wheel of existence

Bhavacakra, the "Wheel of Existence," also called the "Wheel of Life," is one of the most important symbols in the iconographic tradition of the *Vajrayana* and usually decorates the outer wall of a temple, next to the entrance. In a way it illustrates the essence of the "Diamond Vehicle," although it does not represent the teaching itself but the cycle of rebirth that is full of suffering and from which we need to liberate ourselves. Mara, the manifestation of passion and death, is holding the Wheel of Existence in his fangs. Everything that we see inside the wheel was born conditionally and therefore must die—human beings, animals, spirits, the hell realms and the realms of existence of the demi-gods. Even the long-living deities in the uppermost realm of the six realms of existence are still prisoners of the effects of their good actions (*karma*) and their noble intentions. They are also part of the eternally turning wheel of cyclic existence (*samsara*), which those beings keep in motion who have not yet attained enlightenment due to ignorance, desire and hatred. These three poisons, as they are called, are the cause of all suffering in all of the realms of existence and are symbolically depicted as a rooster (desire), a snake (hatred) and a pig (blindness, ignorance).

This is the depiction of the second of the "Four Noble Truths" that the Buddha proclaimed to the world during his famous teachings in Sarnath. Whoever is attached to these fundamental evils is walking the dark path that leads to unhappy and painful situations, as we can see in the second ring from the inside. Whoever takes the path of salvation by following the instructions of the doctrine of the Dharma, is on the path of bliss and will ascend to the enlightened realms.

Whoever is able to recognize the "emptiness" (*sunyata*) of all things, steps onto the hub of the wheel and awakens from the illusions of the world of appearances. Thus, the Buddha is standing outside of the wheel (top right) and is pointing at the full moon to remind us of the night of his enlightenment.

The outer ring illustrates the "conditional birth" in twelve pictures and is read clockwise—death brings about birth, birth brings about conception, conception brings about the willingness to conceive. This willingness to conceive presupposes desire or craving which, in turn, presupposes the possibility of a sensual experience. This brings about sensory organs that are only activated by consciousness and motivation. Yet behind the motivation lies ignorance (*avidya*) which is the ultimate cause of all evils.

101 • *Bhavacakra, the "Wheel of Existence," also called the "Wheel of Life," is an integral part of the canonical iconography of the Buddhist temples.*

Samatha, the meditation path leading to spiritual tranquility

At the bottom right, an adept strives for spiritual tranquility. He has chosen the path of meditation for salvation. Ahead of him we see an elephant and a monkey. The elephant symbolizes the tranquil mind, or wisdom; the monkey symbolizes the restless mind that is constantly jumping back and forth from the past to the future. The latter is not able to conceive a non-dualistic present, the "here and now," in which everything really happens. The not-yet-conscious "wisdom" is making wild leaps to follow the unbridled monkey. Both elephant and monkey are symbolically colored black.

Spurred on by "The Three Precious Jewels" (*Triratna*: Buddha, his teachings and his community), the adept attempts to quieten his mind; the elephant and the monkey are already a reflection of the initial success of his effort. In the third stage the disciple is able to catch "wisdom" with his lasso, which symbolizes memory. The monkey and the elephant turn around in surprise. At the same time a new, temporary inner unrest comes up that is depicted by a hare sitting on the back of the elephant.

In the fourth stage, the adept is able to stand in front of the elephant representing wisdom. He sends the monkey, our constant inner chattering dialogue, to the back of the line. Now the adept has taken the lead. The talkative, restless monkey climbs into a tree to pick the "fruits of virtue" for the adept.

But even this last ruse will not help him. Thoughts remain thoughts; it does not matter how noble they are; they are not needed on the "path to spiritual peace." The restless hare disappears, and shortly afterwards the monkey must also take leave. His feet stay black, since thoughts can never become totally pure. And yet the adept is grateful to him for having helped him discover the power of discernment that is founded on polarity or duality. Duality allows us to realize that there must also be an ultimate polarity in order for duality to be able to exist, namely unity. Thus, the "Great Agreement" has been achieved, the great peace attained. The pure and immaculate, wise elephant is peacefully lying at the feet of the meditating disciple, who is now flying into the highest spiritual realms. The adept becomes wisdom itself in the timeless and spaceless state of pure being. Finally, he enthusiastically comes back riding on the wise elephant to tell the humans about the bliss of nirvana.

102 • *Samatha, the path of meditation.*

The secret tantric path to enlightenment

For the mystics of India the evolution of consciousness takes place in seven stages, in seven different centers. They recognized that *atman*, the cosmic power which brings everything to life, enters our body through the top of our head. There it splits into two poles of energy and flows through the seven energy centers, the seven *chakras*.

Situated at the base (*muladhara*) is the vital, life-giving energy we call sexuality. A tantric starts his work on this level. The formula is "accept, integrate, sublimate." The second chakra (*svadhisthana*) is where our entire digestive system is situated. This chakra also needs to be controlled by specific practices and meditations.

Once the yogi is able to control his two lower chakras, the life force awakens in the third center, in the solar plexus (*manipura*). Here he is in total control of his willpower. In the fourth center, the heart center (*anahata*), the pure energy of love comes to life. Good-heartedness, human warmth and caring is not excessive willpower but a new quality of "divine life force." The anahata chakra is the actual center of man.

The energy continues to flow upward into the thyroid gland (*visuddha*). Whoever awakens in this energy center is on his way to transcending the illusion of "time and space." He becomes an artist, an inventor, a genius. This is the level of creativity.

Finally, in the sixth center or chakra the level of the sage or "prophet" is attained. This chakra (*ajna-chakra*) is associated with the pineal gland; thanks to the "third eye," it makes you clairvoyant. This center is active in children but on an unconscious level. The mechanical figure on the opposite page shows that when this center is active, the base center is asleep. When, during puberty, the root chakra awakens, the center of the childlike, innocent clairvoyance closes. The child becomes an adult, a still unconscious human being who has lost his "innocent childhood." If this level of consciousness is consciously regained through very advanced meditative practices, the "little devils" fall down—as the picture shows—and the yogi, the practicing tantric, the person on the path of salvation, becomes a prophet who heralds the savior or redemption, i.e. enlightenment. The base chakra closes for good. The last stage is the stage of self-realization. In the seventh center, the "thousand-petaled lotus" (*sahasrara*), the state of Enlightenment (*samadhi*) is attained. The life force has come back full circle, but this time consciously, and it cannot be lost again. The seventh and last stage is the stage of God-realization. It is the tantric's path to enlightenment.

103 • Tantric representation of the Seven Chakras or "psychic energy centers."

104 • *Adi-Buddha Samantabhara (all-encompassing good) in the yab-yum (father-mother) posture which symbolizes the mystic union, the highest union of the polarities.*

105 • A rare bronze of the Bodhisattva Chenresig in union with his female counterpart, Prajna. This is also about making something invisible visible: unity. In the figurative sense yab-yum (father-mother) means method (yab) and wisdom (yum). The two together constitute the ultimate fulfillment.

India, the country where the tantric teachings originated

In Tibetan Buddhism tantra is the generic term for the fundamental works of the *Vajrayana*—the *Kangyur* and the *Tengyur*, which literally mean "Translation of the Precepts" (of the Buddha) and "Translation of the Doctrine" (of the Buddha). In this chapter we will not go into these any further, but rather look into the meaning of the concept of tantra and its origin, which is shrouded in mystery. The Indian version of tantra belongs to the fundamental texts of the "Eternal Religions" of India along with the *Vedas*, the *Upanishads*, the *Puranas* and the 6th Book of the *Mahabharata*, the *Bhagavad-Gita*.

The meaning of *sutra* is "thread," the "main connecting thread." The Sanskrit meaning of *tan* is "to stretch," to "complete." Thus, the thread stretches itself into a fabric. In the terminology of the weaver, the crossing thread is called "weft"; the vertical thread is called "warp." Only the weft and the warp together make a fabric. This is a good symbol for the meaning of tantra—the bringing together of polar opposites to create a whole. Everything in our creation is made of polar opposites; tantra tries to bridge the gap between the opposites and to unite them.

The East teaches two totally opposite paths for attaining the state of oneness with our original identity, which, at the same time, is the origin and source of the universe. We are familiar with one of the paths through Christianity and Hinduism—monastic asceticism. The ascetic tries to liberate himself from the fetters of existence through renunciation and castigation. The Buddha also went through this phase on his path to enlightenment, but in vain. The other extreme is tantra, which embraces everything—our emotions, drives, wishes, tendencies and desires—and advises us to live them consciously, in order to release "profound joy" (*mahasukha*) when we reach fulfillment. Tantra is the path of expanding one's consciousness through sensual experiences.

At this point, we are again returning to the vital force in man, to his sexuality. There is hardly any other area in our way of thinking that is as burdened with prejudices, taboos and confused ideas as this one. Fascination and puritanical fear hardly balance one another! Since this ambivalence only exists in the human mind—animals and plants live their sexuality without bias—we should first of all try to use our rational mind to think about what we call sexuality without moral prejudices.

Having taken everything into consideration that was expounded up to now, we have recognized that the entire creation was created out of a kind of original unity that we can call God, nirvana or sunyata. We fell out of the "paradisiacal" state of a dimensionless center, the state of "non-duality" as it is called in the Indian Vedanta philosophy, into "duality," into a world of form in which everything consists of polar opposites—the material world. The Bible teaches us that we were driven out of paradise because we ate from the fruit of the Tree of Knowledge, although that was forbidden; the truth is that man needs the world of the senses and forms to be able to know. But the Buddhist path of salvation invites us to take the "path of knowledge," in order to become whole again, to find the center again. An often quoted tantric text, the *Hevajra Tantra*, says ambiguously, "You have to go through that which can bring your downfall."

When we look around us at the world, we realize that it is governed by movement, movement towards an invisible center. It seems as if our inner momentum were the great longing for the lost self. Every drop of water is looking for the way back to its identity. It falls from the sky, flows as a rivulet, a stream, a river and finally as a mighty river back to the ocean, its maternal source. Every child revolves around the center of its origins, its family, and it longs for motherly security. Even the song of the birds on a clear spring morning sounds like a yearning call, an expression of their desire for unity with a fellow bird.

Isn't it this longing—this ultimately always insatiable yearning for the lost unity that keeps the world in movement—that which we, at the same time, call sexuality? In this dimension sexuality is the vital force that keeps the world going. When tantra talks abut "sexual energy," this vital force—the life-force itself—is meant. Since the fourth century, yogic techniques to consciously work with sexual energy have been developed within both Hinduism and Buddhism.

In the chapter on the "Diamond Vehicle," the two schools have already been described—the "right-hand" school that works with sexual energy only through visualization and the "left-hand" school that sees coitus (*maithuna*) as a secret, sacred ritual. In this connection, we shall briefly talk about the Indian *devadasi* (the temple servants) and the *gotipua* (the "dancing boys").

The "left-hand tantrism" and the tradition of the gotipuas (dancing boys)

Presently in the Indian state of Orissa two dance masters still move around the country with their *gotipuas*, boys disguised as girls who mime the dances of the *devadasi* in front of the temples. This unique tradition has a long historical background. Towards the end of the first millenium, the Bhauma dynasty was governing in the state now called Orissa. The princes of this dynasty built Buddhist monasteries as well as temples of the Shivaite and Shakta-Tantra traditions. Some of the influential princesses considered themselves to be incarnations of Parvati, the wife of Siva, and helped found secret places of tantric initiation. The Princess Hira Mahadevi was supposedly responsible for the construction of the "temple of the 64 yoginis" near the small village of Hirapur.

The temple is circular and opens to the east with an entrance resembling a *yoni* (female sexual organ, considered the cosmic womb), which is guarded on either side by a Siva with an erected phallus. There are 64 niches in the inner circle, in which just as many yoginis demonstrate the "64 postures of pleasure" (Sanskrit: *ratibandha*). As in a mandala, there is a square "palace" in the center which features four walls with a gate in each direction. The "fifth direction," the center, is the "secret place" where the fundamental polarity of everything created dissolves into the "great unity." In the innermost circle of this left-hand tantric place of worship the adept and the devadasi let their male and female "secret places" melt (*maithuna*) into each other, in order to experience the "great bliss" (*mahasukha*) in its highest form.

The palace roof is open to the sky. The couple in the secret center and ritually united by the "secret" creative organs of the human body should not see each other as man and woman, but as the creative male cosmic principle and the receptive female cosmic principle. The physical orgasm represents the path of great bliss that is supposed to lead to the spiritual "great bliss" of oneness with the creative primordial principle.

It is obvious how easily this kind of ritual can be perverted. The devadasi were considered by the general public to be prostitutes. Even contemporary specialist literature hardly makes an effort to look into the spiritual origin of these "left-hand" rituals. They talk lightly about temple prostitution, although neither devadasi nor temples would have been needed for prostitution in the usual sense. Temple dancers or "God-slaves," as the devadasis were also called, were not allowed to perform in public. To satisfy the curiosity of the uninitiated population, someone came up with the droll idea to have these dances imitated by disguised boys whose infantile innocence made them endearing. Only these "angelic" beings were allowed to perform the secret temple dances for the public.

106 • The "temple of the 64 yoginis" near Hirapur in the Indian state of Orissa is one of the rare places of worship where the highly secret so-called "left-hand tantra" initiations took place in the 11th and 12th century. What the Tibetan iconography symbolically presented was practiced here as a temple ritual between the temple dancers (the devadasi) and the adepts.

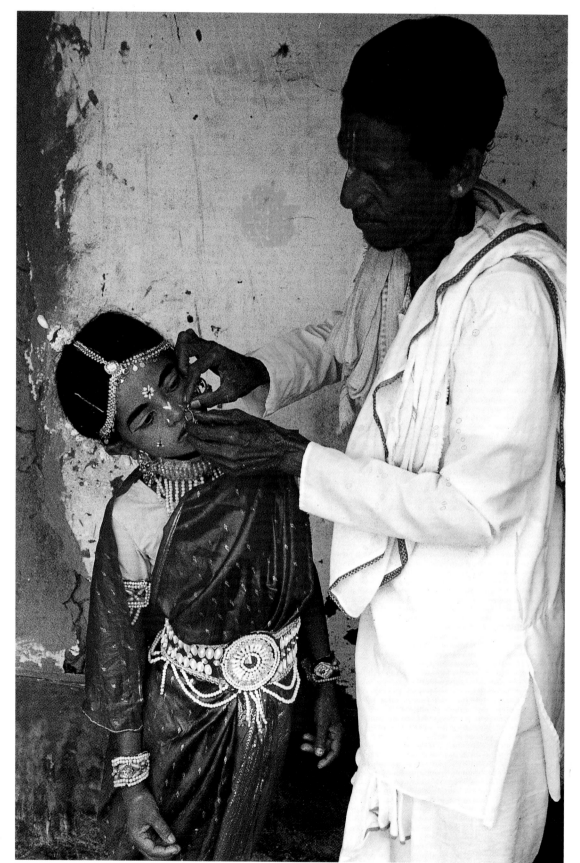

107 • Since the temple dancers were not allowed to perform in public, as they were considered to be prostitutes, the unique tradition of the gotipuas developed. The gotipuas were dancing boys dressed as girls who mimed the secret dances of the devadasis in the temple courtyard. Since the boy-girls are supposed to look like "celestial, sexless beings" and sing with angelic, high voices while they dance, they can only play their roles until puberty. Here the dance master, who was once a gotipua himself, prepares his gotipua for the performance.

108 • *Today there are still two dance masters in Orissa who travel around the country with their two boys, an older and a younger one. The older boy is singing and dancing while the younger one and the dance master watch.*

109 • *Quite demanding acrobatic interludes are part of the performance to keep the public entertained.*

Mandala, the path to the sacred center

The mandala is a symbolic representation of the universe, a "cosmic diagram." Since everything created—and therefore all creatures without exception—is part of the universe, this picture of the cosmos is, at the same time, a portrayal of man in his entire soul structure, a psychogram. In Tibetan a mandala is called *kyil-khor*, which means "center-periphery." Every circle consists of a center and a periphery. While the circumference is defined through space and time—everything that can be experienced through the senses—the center ultimately remains a mystery. The circumference does revolve around the center, but the center itself lies beyond all concepts; it simply is: timeless, spaceless, inconceivable. This mysterious center has always been a symbol for God in all cultures due to its inconceivable perfection. In Tibetan Buddhism it stands for sunyata—the unknown, emptiness, that which has no characteristics, the beginning and end of all being.

Everything springs from the center; everything returns to the center. In its pictorial expression the mandala is a kind of map for understanding the entire universe and, at the same time, for understanding the landscape of our inner selves.

Each person searches for his own path in order to find himself. But the laws of the world, according to which this path runs, remain constant. In spite of their differences, all mandalas are based on the same principles: three circles symbolizing the cosmos surround an earthly, square "palace" that has four gates. The "fifth direction" is in the center where the points of the four triangles converge. Since a mandala is intended to be three-dimensional, the center is the point of a pyramid with a square base. The four angles unite at the top which, consequently, represents the *quinta essentia*, the quintessence of the world and of man. The first circle that man has to cross in order to find himself is made of purifying and transforming fire. Western thought knows the phoenix that rises out of the ashes. Some mandalas that initiate you into the wrathful aspect of a deity feature a field of corpses that must be crossed before you reach the circle of fire (Die or become!).

The second cosmic circle is clear, hard and indestructible like a diamond (*vajra*); it symbolizes the purely spiritual, the "naked mind," as the Tibetans also call it. The third circle, the lotus circle, stands for spiritual rebirth.

The adept is now standing in front of the earthly, square palace with its four gates, which are being guarded by the "guardians of the threshold." It is here that the actual initiation takes place. Depending on the type of mandala, it is led by a "spiritual teacher" (Tibetan: *lama*, Sanskrit: *guru*) and ends with a specific "empowerment" of the adept.

110 • This cosmic mandala can be seen in the courtyard of the Paro-Dzong monastery in western Bhutan. It is a representation of the emergence of the universe, a picture of the first creation of the world. A cosmic whirl is born out of the mysterious "nothing" of the center, and its energy is transmitted outwards like a "shock wave." The emerging shapes of the elements are only suggested in the blue circle. Space is filled with "ether," the seed of all the elements which are still without form. The colored orbits, intersecting with each other concentrically, are revolving around the center. A red aureole of fire closes the mandala to the outside.

111 • *The Vajrabhairava mandala. In this mandala that is supposed to acquaint us with the "wrathful" form of Manjusri, the Bodhisattva of Wisdom, he is depicted in his peaceful form at the top center. If you are initiated into the wrathful aspect of a Bodhisattva, the outer circle that has to be crossed is a field of corpses. Only after that comes the "fire circle," as in all other mandalas, which is followed by the "vajra circle" that is as hard and clear as a diamond. Having crossed the "lotus circle," we are in the inner circle and are standing in front of the palace with its four gates. The gates are guarded by guardians with whom we have to become acquainted before we can approach the center.*

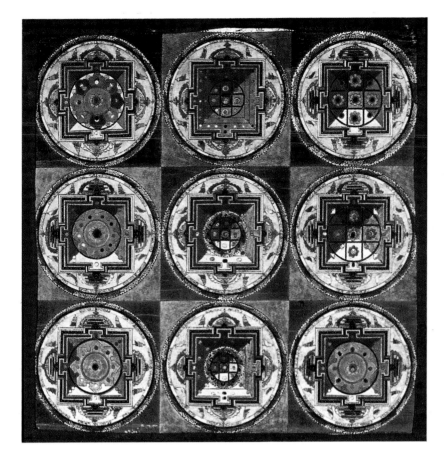

112 • *Nine different mandalas from Paro-Dzong in Bhutan.*

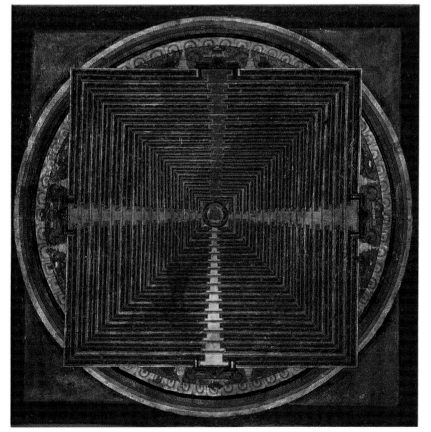

113 • *The Amnata mandala. All mandalas are generally conceived to be three-dimensional. In this case, it is easy to imagine a pyramid seen from above.*

The trikaya doctrine

Early Buddhism was a pure concept of realization. The historical Buddha Sakyamuni taught a method leading to the realization that all phenomena are "empty" in their essence, that everything is changing and flowing, and that this dynamic nature itself is empty of any absolute essence.

In the first phase from Hinayana to Mahayana Buddhism, the great Buddhist thinkers (such as Nagarjuna, the creator of the Madhyamika or "Middle Path," and his disciple Aryadeva) elevated the adjective "empty" (*sunya*) to the substantive "emptiness" (*sunyata*). This way the foundation for a transcendental superstructure, the nihilistic philosophy of sunyavada, was created, which was totally alien to early Buddhism. This transcendental superstructure is reflected in the "trikaya doctrine" ("doctrine of the three bodies"). The *Dharmakaya* ("body of the teaching") corresponds to the earliest conceptions of the Buddha. The Adi-Buddha who is at the top of the pyramid is beyond concepts; he is timeless, immortal, without duality. Unlike the Hinayana view, the latter is considered to be positive (the "emptiness") and not-negative ("empty"). The *Dharmakaya* is attained through wisdom (*prajna*)—through direct insight into the true nature of the world—and is the cosmic consciousness, the Oneness that cannot be conceptualized. The *Sambhogakaya* ("body of joy") is represented as the transcendental Buddha Amitabha who, in the Mahayana tradition, rules in the "Western Paradise." It is an intermediate realm on the path to enlightenment.

On the basis of this assumption, a form of Buddhism has developed in Japan that is not based on the concept that our actions (karma) make us progress, but rather our belief in the Buddha Amitabha. It is called Amidism. In Tibetan Buddhism the Sambhogakaya is occupied by Buddhas and Bodhisattvas in all five directions (the center is counted as an exit for the cardinal directions). As in the case of a mandala, the observer is standing in the east (blue) and looking towards the west (red). The south (yellow) is to the left and the north (green) to the right. The center is white, since it is the point of departure and convergence of all of the colors. The seat of the Bodhisattva Avaloketesvara (Tibetan: *Chenresig*) is in the red west under the Buddha Amitabha; he represents the spiritual principle of the Dalai Lamas. Next to their peaceful aspect, each Buddha and Bodhisattva also has a "wrathful" form and a "peaceful" or "wrathful" counterpart representing the feminine principle (*prajna*). The Buddhist practicing the "Diamond Vehicle" usually chooses one of these many Bodhisattvas as his personal tutelary deity (*yidam*).

The Nirmanakaya, finally, is the "body of transformation," the physical manifestation of the Buddhas and Bodhisattvas in our world. They appear to mankind to fulfill their commitment to lead all beings to liberation.

ADI-BUDDHA

SUNYATA
Emptiness

YIDAM

TRANSCENDENTAL
LEVELS

III. DHARMAKAYA

THE FIVE
TATHAGATA

Amitabha
Ratnasambhava
Vairocana
Amoghasiddhi
Aksobhay

II. SAMBHOGAKAYA

THE
BODHISATTVAS

Avalokitesvara (Chenresig)
Padmapani
Ratnapani
Samantabhadra
Visvapani
Vajrapani

PHYSICAL
LEVELS

I. NIRMANAKAYA

Gautama Buddha (Sakyamuni)

W

"HUMAN-
BODY-
ASPECT"

Kasiapa
S
Krakhuchand
N
Maitreya
O
Kankamuni

The "doctrine of the three bodies" and the symbolism of the number five

In the graph of the "trikaya doctrine," the apex of the pyramid represents the number five. It unifies the square base in itself and constitutes at the same time its point of departure. The apex ends in NOTHINGNESS (*sunyata*), and out of this nothingness, symbolized by the Adi-Buddha, "heaven and earth" come into being, i.e. the transcendental levels, the *Dharmakaya* and *Sambhogakaya* on the one hand, and the earthly plane, the *Nirmanakaya*, on the other hand, emerge.

The languages of the Western cultures still know the expression "quintessence" as the word for the most important part of a thing. The *quinta essentia* (Latin) means "the fifth existing thing." Thus, the later form of Buddhism recognizes five directions by starting with the center and counting that as the "fifth existing entity." There are also five elements (whereas we only know four): earth, water, fire, air and "ether," or "essence"—the "fifth" out of which everything emerges. White is also regarded as the fifth color, as the "quinta essentia," so to speak, of blue, yellow, red and green; consequently, in the iconography, the central place is attributed to it, while each of the primary colors corresponds to one of the directions.

114 • *A Green Tara. In this specific form, she is the "one who saves from the fear of prisons." She is loving and kind and even sends a bird behind the prison walls to undo the bonds of a tormented prisoner.*

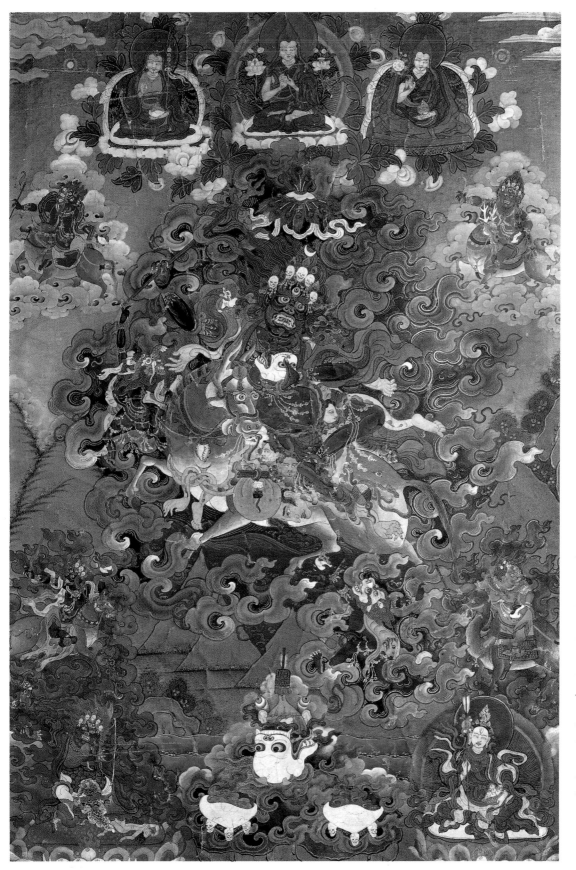

115 • *A kind of shadow of the loving and kind female deities, the wrathful Palden Lhamo is depicted here riding across a sea of blood while sitting on the skins of children and spreading the plague. Wherever there is light there is also shadow! Tibetan Buddhism makes us aware of this fact over and over again. Only when we know the shadow, have made friends with it and invoke it as a protective deity, can we know the entire truth and be liberated. Palden Lhamo is the protective deity of Lhasa.*

116 • A red dakini in the form of Kacho Wangmo. She is sort of a celestial fairy from pre-Buddhist times. By exposing her feminine charms, she stimulates the sexual instincts in order to send these energies through the heavenly spheres to one of the transcendental Buddhas to whom she has special access.

117 • *Wearing the mask of a wild snow lion and surrounded by an aureole of flames, the red dakini races through the cosmic realms in the form of Sengdong-ma. Because she is disguised as a demon, she is protected from real demons while on her journey! The deeper meaning here is also the achieving of unity through the joining of polarities.*

118 • *The Bodhisattva Padmapani, the "Lotus-Born One." He embodies karuna, loving kindness and active compassion for all "sentient beings." He is a form of Avaloketesvara (Tibetan:* Chenresig) *who is highly venerated in Mahayana Buddhism. The Dalai Lamas are embodiments of this Bodhisattva. "Pity and active compassion" make up the path, and prajna, the "realization of the highest wisdom," is the goal.*

119 • *Manjusri is the Bodhisattva of wisdom and therefore one of the most important figures of the Buddhist pantheon. If Padmapani is the path, then Manjusri is the goal. Here he is depicted riding a snow lion. He is usually shown with a sword that he uses to cut through ignorance. The wrathful aspect of Padmapani is the "Great Black One" (Mahakala), and the wrathful aspect of Manjusri is the buffalo-headed Yamantaka who is shown on the following page.*

120 • The negative counterpart of the wise Manjusri is Yamantaka, the Terrible. He has several buffalo heads and is raging in an ocean of flames to put an end to the "Lord of Death." At the top, above his horns, it is comforting to perceive the face of his peaceful aspect.

The Tibetan Book of the Dead

"Just as of all the footprints those of the elephant are the biggest, so of all the meditations on awareness the one on death is the most sublime" (from the sutra on Buddha's entry into parinirvana).

Certain secret Tibetan teachings deal with the state between the physical death of a person and his new earthly existence. These scriptures, which date back to the 8th century and whose importance has only been recognized to its full extent during the last few years by scholars doing research on death, are probably some of the most valuable texts the Eastern traditions have given to humanity. *The Tibetan Book of the Dead* probably belongs to the "hidden scriptures" (*terma*) that were rediscovered in the 14th century. They are ascribed to the great sage Padmasambhava. The first German translation was published in 1935. In a preface to the book, C.G. Jung writes the following. "The philosophy of the Bardo Thodol is the quintessence of Buddhist psychological criticism and as such—it may be stated here—vastly superior."

Bardo means "between two" or "intermediate stage," and *thodol* means "liberation through hearing." The Bardo Thodol is actually a book of mysteries that gives us step-by-step instructions on how we should conduct ourselves during the intermediate stage between death and rebirth in order to attain the ultimate liberation.

The journey into the hereafter starts with the last breath. The spiritual master (lama) sitting next to the dying person observes how "the earth element sinks into the water, how the water element evaporates in the fire, how the fire element disappears into air, how the air element dissolves into empty space." At the end of this process, the person has breathed his last and left his physical body. The dangerous journey through the intermediate stage (bardo) that takes 49 days has begun. The human being who has been separated from his physical body regains consciousness after having been unconscious for a short—or longer—period of time. He "awakens" in the bardo and feels as if he is in control of his senses. This state is comparable to our dream state when we can see, hear, feel, smell and taste without being aware that we are dreaming. Likewise, *The Tibetan Book of the Dead* assumes that the deceased person cannot perceive his new state right away.

Now the spiritual helper, sitting close to the corpse, starts imparting the teachings to the deceased and initiates him into existence in the bardo. Unlike the initiations given to the living, which utimately all focus on death, this initiation prepares for rebirth. Whereas the initiations on earth lead you from the outside to the inside or from below to above, the journey into the hereafter starts with the perception of the "Great Primordial Light" and then gradually spirals downwards into illusion and clouding of the consciousness until it finally ends in a new maternal womb. Thus the lucid climax of the human being is death. The moment of death is, as strange as it may sound, the climax of life.

"Oh, noble one, listen!" says the lama at this point to the deceased. "Now you experience the rays of the 'clear light' of true reality. Recognize it! Oh, noble one, your present mind—which is empty according to its true nature, which has neither characteristics nor color—is naturally empty, is the true reality." If the dead person were able to objectively remain "in the emptiness of the abundance of the light and therefore step onto the hub of the Wheel of Rebirth," as Jung puts it, the ultimate liberation would be attained.

But anyone who has not already learned during his lifetime to melt with this "clear light" in his meditative practices, to give up the illusionary limitations of the "I" and to dissolve into the "abundance of light that knows neither birth nor death," will now be terrified and close his eyes. The "clear light" unleashes a state of panic-stricken fear of total annihilation or disintegration. No belief system, no philosophy will be of any help now; we need to recognize beforehand that there is no "self," no "I," that this center which we call "I" is empty. Thus the "wanderer in the hereafter" clings to an illusionary "I," and the "clear light" takes on the form of illusionary celestial beings. Our spiritual helper points out to us over and over again that we are projecting our own subjective images, similar to our dream images when we sleep at night.

After seven days of attempting in vain to recognize the true nature of these celestial hierarchies, the images begin to get darker as the deities start to appear in their wrathful forms. The deceased had the opportunity to prepare himself for these encounters while he was alive. A meditation practice that fits this situation is described in *The Book of the Dead*: "Whoever your tutelary deity may be, meditate over its form for a long time and see it as being apparent but not really existing, like a figure evoked by a magic spell. Then, let the visualization of your tutelary deity dissolve by starting with the extremities until nothing of it is left to be seen, and put yourself in the state of clarity and emptiness—something you cannot imagine as being concrete—and remain in this state for a while. Then meditate on the 'clear light' again. Do this alternately. Afterwards allow your own intellectual mind to gradually melt away, starting with your extremities." The text shows that the images that appear in the bardo state are dream images. Just as in a dream, we can only relativize these apparitions when we are awake; only then are we able to realize that they were dream images.

After seven more days, the journey into the hereafter continues and ends in the death realm. Yama, the Lord of Death, holds a mirror in front of us, that makes us aware of our actions, and this is the most cruel torture. We can still hear the voice of our spiritual guide from afar who reminds us: "Oh, noble wanderer in the hereafter"—and our name follows—"realize that you have no head that can be chopped off, no skin that can be peeled off a living body. Realize this and you can attain liberation at this moment!" But it is already too late. We no longer have the energy. We are only driven by the wish to awaken. With all our heart we wish for a new physical body. We are pervaded by wild sexual fantasies. We observe couples living together and are on the lookout for a maternal womb.

Thus begins a new cycle, a new life on earth, a new hope. Maybe we will realize this time around that samsara, the cycle of birth and death, and nirvana, "the great peace," are not different worlds but reflections of the One Reality.

Explanations for the graphic representation of the "Bardo Thodol"

This drawing is an attempt to illustrate samsara, the cycle of birth and death. What strikes us when we look at the graph is that life is not the opposite of death, but that birth is the opposite of death, and that a "life with a body" is the opposite of a "life without a body." On the side of the "life with a body," i.e. our earthly existence, we differentiate between three intermediate stages or bardos:

(1) The Nirmanakaya that lasts from the moment our physical body is infused with life until it leaves the body at the time of death and includes the experiences of our waking consciousness.

(2) The Sambhogakaya that lasts from the moment we fall asleep until we wake up in the morning and includes the world of our nighttime dreams.

(3) The Dharmakaya that means the beginning and end of a meditation. Once we have attained the highest possible state in meditation, i.e. "consciousness without content," called samadhi in the Eastern terminology, we look into the "clear light."

The moment we cross the threshold of death, shortly after the "great passing away," we are confronted with that which is called "clear light" (*chi-kha'i-bardo*) in *The Tibetan Book of the Dead*. Only the person who has learned during his lifetime to give up the illusory existence of the ego in order to lose himself in the ALL-ONE, will now have the courage to meet the "clear light" face to face. Only the saint will not have to avert his eyes from this "divine light."

For all beings who are still caught in samsara, the descent into the *chonyid-bardo*, during which we experience the "reality of the doctrine" just as real as in a dream, starts now. All of the celestial hierarchies that we dealt with during our lifetime will appear to us now. First they take on their most lucid form, and then they appear in more and more wrathful forms.

Finally, the burning desire arises in us to escape from this realm, which is called the *sidpa-bardo* in *The Book of the Dead*. Our most ardent wish is to wake up. Erotic images and wild sexual fantasies torment us. We are attracted by the vibrations of cohabitating couples, we watch them and fall in love with the future mother, if we are a male, or with the future father, if we are a female. We once again enter into a new cyclic existence. Our consciousness descends into a maternal womb, a new day on earth begins.

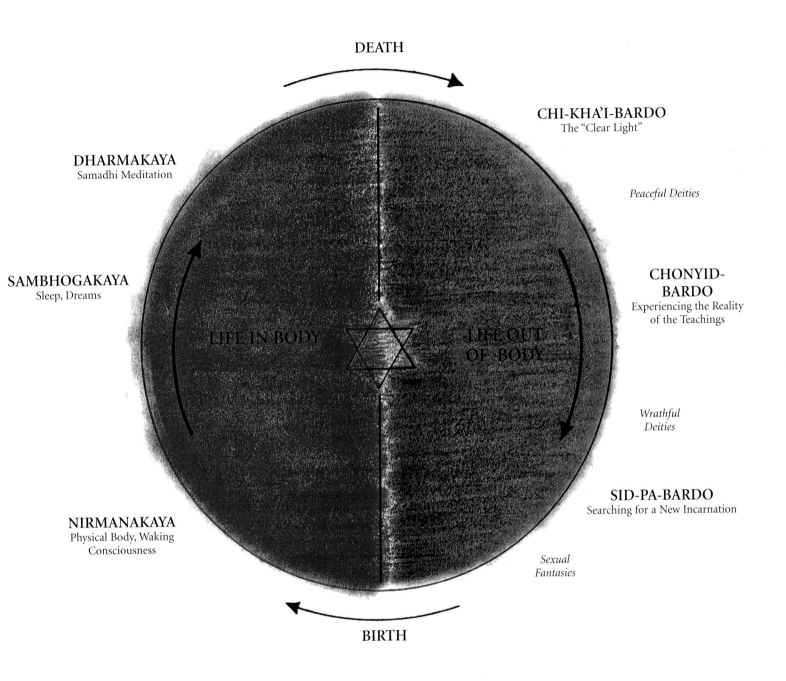

DEATH

DHARMAKAYA
Samadhi Meditation

SAMBHOGAKAYA
Sleep, Dreams

NIRMANAKAYA
Physical Body, Waking
Consciousness

LIFE IN BODY

LIFE OUT
OF BODY

CHI-KHA'I-BARDO
The "Clear Light"

Peaceful Deities

CHONYID-
BARDO
Experiencing the Reality
of the Teachings

*Wrathful
Deities*

SID-PA-BARDO
Searching for a New Incarnation

*Sexual
Fantasies*

BIRTH

The Bardo States

121 • Here Dorje-chang-Chenpo, the "great holder of the dorje," is standing in for all the peaceful deities whom the "wanderer in the hereafter" meets during the first part of his journey.

122 • The Dharmaraja Yamantaka, surrounded by a fire aureole, is supposed to represent the nightmarish experiences that the "wanderer in the hereafter" has. Happy is the man who has confronted and made peace with his dark elemental forces during his lifetime; he does not have to fear them now!

123 • *Yama, the Lord of Death, holds a mirror in front of our eyes to make us aware of our actions. We are under the impression that we are experiencing the most atrocious torments. The "wanderer in the hereafter" hardly hears the voice of the guiding lama sitting next to him, who reminds him to realize that everything is only a projection, "images from your heart." We only have one wish: to wake up.*

124 • The journey into the Bardo comes to an end. The desire to have a new existence becomes overpowering. The "wanderer in the hereafter" is reminded to choose a maternal womb that will lead to a good reincarnation. He tunes in to the vibration of couples living together and finally finds his new parents in this way.

A new day dawns. Once again, the perfection of the bud is determined in advance. Once again, we are given the opportunity to let it blossom, to let it open itself to the light. "Om mani padme hum." Will we succeed this time?

> *You live in illusion and in the world of appearances*
> *but there is a reality.*
> *You are this reality, but you do not know it.*
> *When you awaken to this reality you will realize that you are nothing,*
> *and that in being nothing you are everything.*
>   (Kalu Rinpoche)

Dialogue: conversation between a master and a disciple

M —Who are you?
D —That is what I am searching for.

M —Sit down next to me. Since when have you been occupying yourself with spiritual
 things?
D —Since my childhood.

M —What have you done for your development?
D —Life has presented me with challenges; then I practiced yoga under the guidance of an
 Indian master. I also meditate.

M —So you practiced yoga. Which form of meditation did you choose?
D —The apparently simplest one. In India it would probably be called "Vipassana."

M —And what did you find out in the past thirty years that you did not know at the time
 you started?
D —(After hesitating a while) That I am "I."

M —Were you not already "I" thirty years ago?
D —Yes, of course!

M —How much effort did it take to be "I" at that time?
D —None, I just was...

M —Why did you then look for something that you have always been?
D —?

M —When you sleep, do you also exist?
D —Certainly!

M —And does it take an effort?
D —No, I cannot make any effort when I am asleep.

M —Who inside you knows that you also exist in your sleep?
D —There is something like a constant observer in us who is always awake, who observes
 even in our sleep, who observes our dreams, for instance.

M —That is very important. But as soon as you think about this observer, he is already part of your mind!

D —I am aware of that. But when I talk, I have to express myself through words.

M —Who in you is observing the difficulty of putting things in words?

D —He observes silently.

M —No words?

D —No, no words. Maybe a Zen koan, "the noise of the clapping of a hand."

M —Yes—"Non-duality"—Silence…
  (After a while) What made the greatest impression on you in your life?

D —Looking into the eyes of an enlightened master.

M —That is inspiration, but it is still on the physical level. (After a moment of silence) What will you do now?

D —After everything that I have experienced up to now, there is really nothing to do.

M —Yes, but how can you do "nothing"?

D —When we want everything that happens, doesn't everything happen that we want to happen? What then is left to do? Maybe only the most difficult thing is left to do: to let go of all our desires. Our desires keep us attached to this world.

M —All of our desires? (He asks insistently.) Even the wish to attain enlightenment some day?

D —Yes, all of our wishes; even our wish for enlightenment.